LOOKING BACK AT HEWORTH A YORK SUBURB

by
Avril E. Webster Appleton

ISBN 0 9536257 0 2

Published by
Avril E. Webster Appleton
18 Whitby Drive, York, England, YO31 1EX
Telephone 01904 424872

Printed by
J. W. Bullivant & Son
296 Bishopthorpe Road, York, YO23 1LG
Telephone 01904 623241 Facsimile 01904 621670

C O N T E N T S

Front Cover: Heworth Village, Circa 1920s. Courtesy of J. Murphy.

Back Cover: OS MAP 1893. Crown Copyright.

Inside Front and Back Cover: OS MAP 1909. Crown Copyright.

FOREWORD

Little did I think all those years ago when I started a W.E.A. class on a study of Heworth history, many of the discoveries made in the course of research would be written up and published by one of my first students. Avril has stuck to local history through thick and thin, studying palaeography and taking a Local History Certificate at the University of York, as well as coping with all the vicissitudes of her family life. All through those years we have kept in touch and I have followed her activities with interest, her trips to Spain, the publication of her book on Layerthorpe and her growing number of speaking engagements. The idea of producing a book based on her own experiences as a Heworth resident has inspired this latest volume and is backed by an introduction to the much earlier history of what was one of York's smallest suburban villages. She has diligently followed up every lead; looked at all the original documents and spun the whole into a fascinating story, which turns into a positive cornucopia of delights for this century.

I wish her book every success and may it provide an inspiration for others.

Jennifer Kaner, B.Sc.
W.E.A. Lecturer.

INTRODUCTION

With the onset of the new Millennium, I decided to write about a suburb of York I was very familiar with, Heworth. Heworth sprang up as a separate village, 1 mile from the centre of York. After the Enclosure of Heworth Moor in 1822, the village began to develop and spread out until it became a suburb of York. The main village street, where some of the oldest cottages are situated, is still called Heworth Village. The Shoulder of Mutton and the Nag's Head, two old public houses, are still well patronised and the Victorian church school is still in use. Many interesting and important people have lived in Heworth through the ages and it's history has been irrevocably bound up with the history of York. I came to Heworth in 1941 and for nearly sixty years have lived in that area. It gives me great pleasure to be able to write about people and places I remember from my childhood and also to include my own, my brother's, and my parent's memories. Unfortunately it is impossible to include everyone who has ever lived in Heworth and I apologise to anyone who thinks they should have had a mention.

I dedicate this book to anyone who has had any connections with Heworth and to my Mum and Dad, Mr. and Mrs. A. T. Reeder, now alas deceased, but who gave me and my brother David, lots of happy memories of a Heworth childhood.

Avril E. Webster Appleton

ACKNOWLEDGEMENTS

My thanks go to all that have helped me with this book. To my daughter Ann and son in law Bernie for their help in the early stages and to my son David for his help in the later stages. To my husband Cliff and all my family for all their help, encouragement and understanding. To Rita and all staff at York City Archives and Amanda and staff at York Reference and Tang Hall libraries. Also the Borthwick Institute and North Riding Record Office. To Mr. David Poole for all his help and information and Mr. Joe Murphy for the loan of photographs.

A special thanks must go to Mrs. Jennifer Kaner, who is always ready to give help and encouragement and whose W. E. A. local history classes gave me the initial inspiration to research. Grateful thanks must also go to all those past and present Heworth residents, who have loaned photographs and given valuable information and to everyone who has helped to make this publication possible.

Avril E. Webster Appleton

CHAPTER I
EARLY TIMES

The name Heworth is Anglo-Saxon and means a High Enclosure.[1] In Pre-Roman times the Heworth area was mostly a boggy waste with Birch and Aspen. The small settlement, which was situated along the street, now still, called Heworth Village, was on higher ground. Remains of flints, possibly from an Iron Age farm were found in the Walney Road area. An Anglo Saxon burial ground was discovered in the Pottery Lane, Heworth Green area in 1879.[2]

Roman Remains
The Romans came to York in AD71 and for more than three hundred years were garrisoned at the town then called Eboracum. One of the first acts of the Roman Commander would be to see that his field army, mostly cavalry and supply wagons, could move easily and rapidly to the East Yorkshire Coast and other forts, so Roman roads were laid down. In the summer of 1959, during drainage works, a hitherto unknown Roman road was found at Appletree Farm, Bad Bargain Lane. Traces of this road were also unearthed at Ryethorpe Grange near Cow Moor Bridge, down Stockton Lane. Burials were also found alongside the road near Appletree farm which consisted of, one lead coffin in a wood lined grave and two stone sarcophagi. They all contained remains of skeletons. Roman pottery and tiles were also found in this area, implying some sort of habitation, perhaps a villa. Traces of this road and Roman coins were also found when the Ashley Park Estate was built. A Roman cemetery had been discovered in 1878 off Heworth Green, Dodsworth Avenue area, when the Foss Islands Railway was built. The Romans usually buried their dead along the sides of the major roads into York. The richest classes seemed to have been buried along the Tadcaster Road. In Heworth, cinary urns, stone and wood coffins and large communal pits for slaves and people of ill repute were discovered.[3]

The Norman Conquest
Before the Norman Conquest, Orm, son of Gamel and Watheof, son of Siward, Earl of Northumberland, held Heworth, Orm was in the service of King Harold and was said to have been slain by Tostig, Harold's brother, at the Battle of Stamford Bridge. After the Battle of Hastings, William 1st of Normandy was crowned King of England in 1066. In 1068, William came north to quell the uprisings of the old Saxon lords and much land was laid to waste. This was called "The Harrowing of the North".

The first official record was the Domesday Survey of 1086. After the Conquest, Hugh son of Baldric was granted three carucates of land in Heworth (one

1

carucate was roughly 120 acres) The Count of Mortain, William's brother, three carucates, and Earl Alan of Richmond another three. William gave land to his family and thanes for help in the war, but these lands were scattered about so the Lords would not become too powerful. The Count of Mortain, granted his land to Richard Surdival and Nigel Fossard of Huntington. St. Mary's Abbey at York acquired land in Heworth and one carucate of land at Monk Bridge. Earl Alan gave his land to St. Saviour's Parish. Hugh, son of Baldric gave some of his land to the Fitzalan family and some to St. Mary's Abbey. Six bovates of land went to the Marmion family who owned West Tanfield near Masham.[4]

The Langton Family
The first York man to become lord of the Manor of Heworth was Nicholas Langton in 1316. His father, Nicholas Langton senior, was lord Mayor of York 1297-1306. They were merchants in York who, when they became rich, bought land around York and became the first landed gentry. Nicholas Langton junior also became lord Mayor of York in 1322-1333. In 1322, the Archbishop appointed him Keeper of his Palace and Prison in York. He became lord of the Manor of Heworth in 1316 but whether he actually lived in Heworth was a matter of some conjecture. He also owned a mill at Tang Hall Bridge, then called Thief Bridge, which he rented from the Prebend of Fridaythorpe and was the richest inhabitant in Heworth in 1301. There were forty-six people in Heworth paying tax in the Poll Tax of 1377. The Langton family held the Manor of Heworth for the next 100 years until Agnes Langton, the heiress to the Langton fortune, married James Danby Esq. of Thorpe Perrow. James Danby was knighted by Richard III. His son Christopher married the daughter of Lord Scrope and inherited lands at Masham.[5] In 1568 the Danby family wished to consolidate their estate at Masham, so they sold their Manor of Heworth to Elizabeth Kellett, widow of a corn merchant of York. It consisted of eight messuages (houses), six cottages and one water mill. Elizabeth Kellett had two daughters, Jane and Elizabeth. Jane married Thomas Thwenge, a lawyer in the York courts and Elizabeth married Lancelot Foster. Elizabeth Kellett left her Heworth estate to Jane and Thomas Thwenge and sold Hall Fields, which was land near Layerthorpe, and some property along the Stray to Robert Askwith a prosperous York Draper, Alderman and M.P. for York.[6]

Heworth Moor
Heworth Moor, which was not enclosed until 1822, was a large tract of land, which stretched from Monk Bridge over most of Heworth Township to Sandburn down Malton Road. There were two boundary crosses on the Moor. The first was near the junction of Malton Road and Stockton Lane and was known as "The Cross on the Moor". It had originally been a wooden cross, but in the 16th century became a stone boundary stone. The other cross was at the

present Heworth Road and East Parade. The Moor was used to pasture York citizen's cattle and sheep. It was also used for assemblies, military parades and shooting practice for the Militia.[7] In the time of the War of the Roses, skirmishes often took place between the Percy family and the Nevilles, in Yorkshire. They both held land in the Vale of York. The Percy family holding Spofforth and Topcliffe, and the Nevilles, Sheriff Hutton, Elvington and Middleham. One such battle or skirmish which previously had been placed at Stamford Bridge, according to new evidence provided by a leading historian, could have taken place on Heworth Moor. It was said that 5, 000 Percy tenants and York craftsmen laid in wait on Heworth Moor for a Neville wedding party returning to Sheriff Hutton from Lincolnshire. However, there is still some dispute as to whether this conflict can rightly be called a battle or just a skirmish or whether there was any bloodshed or any slain.[8]

There were at least three windmills on the Moor in 1734. One had been owned and leased out by the Corporation in the 16th century. A windmill was referred to in 1746, when W. Farrar agreed to pay £7 for materials of an old mill on Heworth Moor. "It should be pulled down, being very ruinous and situated near the highway to be a nuisance." A windmill stood at the junction of Glen Road and Harcourt Street in 1850, the miller then was John Asquith. No trace of this mill now remains. Somewhere near the Moor, probably on the north of Heworth Green was some ground called "Keble Flak" In 1575, Mrs. Dawson of Heworth Grange, was told to "Clean the sewer which came from Keble Flaks, through the Grange Fields, which drowneth the Moor so the kyne (cattle) cannot pass to the pasture".[9]

In 1642, King Charles 1st withdrew from Parliament after months of dispute and set up his headquarters in York. One hundred and thirty six men were said to have camped on Heworth Moor. In June 1642, he summoned all householders to the Moor where it was reported there had been a gathering of sixty to eighty thousand people. The Civil War was declared in August 1642. In February 1643, news reached York that Queen Henrietta Maria had arrived at Bridlington from Holland. An escort was sent to conduct her to York and she was met on Heworth Moor by the Lord Mayor, aldermen and a great welcoming crowd of citizens. The Queen brought with her considerable quantities of ordnance and ammunition. She stayed three months in York before joining her husband at Oxford. In 1644, the Parliamentarian army besieged York. Seven windmills were burnt on Heworth Moor and Layerthorpe and Monk Bridges were destroyed.[10]

HEWORTH WINDMILL
This windmill stood on the junction of Glen Road and Harcourt Street. Demolished about 1890. *(Courtesy of Miss K. Hayes)*

Chapter I. Notes and References.

1. K. Cameron. *English Place Names.* London. (1961) p148.
2. W. Page. (ed) Victoria County History. *History of Yorkshire 11.* 103
3. Yorkshire Philosophical Society. *Annual Reports.* 1966-1973. 44-60.
4. J. Morris. (ed) *Domesday Book.* Chichester (1986) p1 298. b. c.
5. P. M. Tillot. (ed) Victoria County History. *The City of York.* (1961) 112. Additional information. Mrs. J. Kaner, 77 Stockton Lane.
6. Yorkshire Archaeological Record Series. *Yorkshire Fines. 11.* (1567). V. 308. 340. Vol III (1584/5) p 32.
7. P. M. Tillot. (ed) op. cit. 5. 286.
8. J Kaner. *Battle of Heworth Moor.* Y.A.Y.A. Times. (1982) No. 7 p 8-10.
9. York Reference Library. (subsequently referred to as Y.R.L.) Raine, A. *Medieval York.* J Murray. (1955) pp. 284. 285.
10. Knight, C. B. *History of York.* Herald Printers (1944) p.454.

CHAPTER II
CATHOLICS AND THE CIVIL WAR

Early Farmers

The little we know about the early farmers in Heworth can only be gleaned from documents such as subsidy rolls, poll taxes, early wills and parish registers. From a Subsidy Roll of 1544, in the time of Henry VIII, we can see who were the wealthiest families in Heworth then. These were the Waites, Vause, Beeforth and Groves families.[1] The Township of Heworth in these early times fell into the jurisdiction of three parishes, St. Saviours, All Hallows, later St. Cuthberts and St. Olaves. Many farmers lived in their farmhouses, which was in one parish but kept their sheep in fields which lay in another parish. Many disputes arose about which church the tythes of lambs and wool would be paid. In a tythe case of 1540, Heworth farmers, Richard Addyson, Robert Buttes, John Groves, Thomas Vause and William Awgur are mentioned.[2]

Field Names

A little more information about Elizabethan and Georgian times in Heworth can be obtained from old deeds, church terriers and wills. Many of the old field names are mentioned in these documents. In Heworth village street in the 16th & 17th centuries, there was the Pinfold, Ash Tree Garth, where the Methodist Chapel and adjoining houses now stand, Walnut Tree Garth, where the Walnut Tree public house is and Penny Garth and Martin Garth adjoining. Behind these garths, or enclosed areas of land, was Paradise Close, where Paradise Cottage stood until the 1960's, and Long Garth behind. At the bottom end of the village was Parsonage Croft, land owned by St. Cuthbert's Church and where the St. Cuthbert's Rectory was, the Victorian building is still there but now flats. On the other side of the village there was Well's Garth, Britton's Garth and Pale Garth, near the old Britannia Inn. The area near the beck (called then the Foss Beck) was called the Holmes, Branch Crofts was near Bad Bargain Lane, as was Foss Butts and Silver Pools. Down Hempland Lane was the Hemplands and off Stockton Lane, Westlands and Northlands. The area where Whitby Avenue is was called Ashlands or Eshlands and Whitby Drive, Swarthmoor Close. Near Cow Moor Bridge was the Cow Moors and the New Moors. Hallfields was in Layerthorpe and Vicar's leas owned by the Vicar's Choral, was near Mill Lane. The Grange Fields stretched up to Monk Bridge and over to Muncaster.[3]

In 1715, in a Registration of Catholic Estates, William Thwenge was said to possess the "Manor of Heworth with Court Leek, capital messuage with barn, two frontisteads and two gardens. Hall Garth and Ashlands, 11 acres in New Moors, 6 pasture gates in the Cow Moors and ground called Holmes with a cottage standing on it".[4] In 1678, Edward Thwenge sold some of his Heworth

5

property to John Agar of Stockton. "Two closes called Branchcrofts and part of a close called Little Holme. A messuage and garth called Pecket Garth and Walnut Tree Garth and a toft called Wells Garth on which there was an ancient messuage and one close, Lasenby Close, occupied by Richard Avison". This would be cottages and land in Heworth Village.[5]

Wills

A little more information about life in Tudor and Elizabethan times can be gleaned from wills. In 1546, in the time of Henry VIII, John Waite of Heworth left to his nephew George Waite "£10 and my best gown and doublet with satin sleeves". To his daughter Elizabeth he left £6, to Richard Cowterde his best jacket, Agnes his sister, one quie with calf and John Gawgresan, one old "graie" mare.[6]

Richard Dawson, who died in 1602, left the lease of the Grange Fields and lease of his new dwelling house at Heworth to his wife. He left also "To John Dawson, a branded whie, "and to each of his servants a sheep. Mari Dawson, his wife, who died twelve years later, left to her son Richard, £400, and to her son William £40. She said in her will that she forgave the debts of Richard Newbie, her son in law, but only gave his wife Elizabeth (her daughter) £10 and refused to give her more. Obviously there had been a family fall out here.[7] Many of the Heworth families intermarried. Richard Dawson married Mari Thwenge, William Dawson married Mary Agar. John Agar married Elizabeth Waite and John Vause married Jennett Addison and their daughter Elizabeth married Thomas Lasenby.[8] In 1700, William Thwenge left to his son William, "The Manor house I now dwell in called Heworth Hall, my messuage house called Pearson's Wife House and my Cottage called Ibbitsons. My wife shall enjoy for her life one parlour; two closets and the two chambers over them belonging to my messuage called Pearson's Wife's House". In 1632 Martha Clapham of Beamsley, Richard Dawson's mother in law left to her daughter Elizabeth, "The white maire I usually ride on, my best gown, kirtle and bodice also my best black velvet gown with russett satin bodice. To my grandaughter Martha Dawson, a pair of linen sheets and two pillow cases, my best gloves and one little trunk now at Heworth".[9]

The Thwenge Family

The Thwenge or Thwing family, who acquired the Manor of Heworth in 1597 were Catholics. They were related to the Thwenges of Upper Helmsley and Kilton Castle in Cleveland. They married into the powerful Catholic Gascoigne and Vavascour families. They were constantly being presented in the Quarter Sessions for their religion and fined. When Henry VIII broke away from Rome he declared himself the Supreme Head of the Church in England because the

Pope refused to agree to his divorce from Katherine of Aragon to marry Anne Boleyn. After the turbulence of the Reformation, Elizabeth 1st, introduced a new religious settlement and decreed that everyone must attend the Anglican Church, swear an oath of Allegiance to the Sovereign as Head of the Church or be liable to be fined. Most people conformed, but a small group, preferring to cling onto their old Catholic faith, refused to attend Church and said masses instead in their own homes. They were known as Catholic Recusants. The Thwenge family was one of these.

These Catholic families were also severely fined or imprisoned if caught harbouring Jesuit priests. In 1592, Anthony Page, a Catholic priest was caught hiding in an out house at Heworth Manor House. Anne Thwenge was committed to prison instead of her brother William. In 1600, Edward Thwenge, a priest, was executed at Lancaster Castle.[10]

In 1681, Edward Thwenge, another priest, son of George Thwenge of Heworth was executed at York. He had been caught up in the Titus Oates plot. His remains were interred in St. Mary's Castlegate but his vestments are now at the Bar Convent. His uncle Sir Thomas Gascoigne aged 85 was also tried in London at this time but acquitted. He was accused of plotting against the King and trying to establish a nunnery in Heworth.[11]

One branch of the Thwenge family lived in the old Manor House, now demolished, which was situated at the corner of the now Walney Road, opposite the Walnut Tree public house. Mr. Thwenge's old house, Heworth Hall, had probably been in this area also. Most of the Heworth inhabitants of this time lived down the village street, which stretched from Dales Lane to Hempland Lane.

Mary Ward

Born at Mulwith Manor near Ripon in 1585, Mary Ward, although she had originally entered the Order of Poor Clares in St. Omer, decided to start a religious community herself, whose members would teach but would not be enclosed. She travelled extensively through Europe hoping for the Pope's blessing to open schools, where girls could be educated. However Mary's requests were too novel, she was a woman three centuries ahead of her time. After having little success in Rome she eventually returned to England and her native Yorkshire. She came to Heworth in 1639, just before the start of the Civil War and lived in a house in the village provided by the Thwenges.[12] The Civil War began in 1642. York was garrisoned by the Royalists and gentry families from surrounding areas moved into the city. Mary Ward, before she left Heworth, placed two statues, one of St. Michael and one of St. Joseph, at each end of the village to safeguard it from the Parliamentarians. However four hundred Roundhead soldiers were reported to have been billeted in the village.

York was besieged in 1644 and after the battle of Marston Moor it finally surrendered. Mary Ward, although very ill at this time returned to Heworth. It was said that Heworth was "To ill to receive her, all the lead off the houses, all the iron from the windows and doors, full of stink and vermin, four hundred soldiers beside the sick having lodged therein. In the gardens they had buried diverse of their soldiers, the whole air so infected as in the whole village there were not three well. All that was delightful taken away, the lovely trees cut down, the gardens unpaled and wholly ruinated".[13]

Mary died in Heworth in 1645, but as a Catholic was denied burial in consecrated ground, so she was buried secretly at Osbaldwick by a Minister who was "honest enough to be bribed". Although Mary died with her aims unfulfilled her work was carried on. Nearly forty years after her death Frances Bedingfield, one of her companions returned to York where she founded the Bar Convent School. A plaque to Mary Ward's memory is in St. Thomas's Church Osbaldwick. Every year, nuns make the annual pilgrimage from Heworth, down Metcalfe's lane, to Osbaldwick Church. Her remains are now in the Bar Convent Museum.[14]

HEWORTH MANOR HOUSE This old Manor House stood at the end of Walney Road, opposite the Walnut Tree public house. Demolished in the 1920's.

(Courtesy of City of York Library)

Chapter II. Notes and References.

1. Public Record Office. E179. 1544/5.
2. Y.R.L. Y.A.S. Rec. Series. (cxlv)Tithe Cause. 9-16. RV. 11G. 298.
3. York City Archives. (subsequently referred to as Y.C.A.) St. Saviour's Church Assessments, AC, 95. 1716-1746. St. Olave's Churchwarden's Accounts. 1753. N.R. Register of Deeds. AM 367 473.(1763)
4. Y. R. L. Rev. J. T. Atkinson(ed) N.R.R.O. Quarter Sessions Returns. Registration of Papist's Estates. 26.
5. Y.C.A. 113/11. (1678)
6. Borthwick Institute of Historical Research. Will of John Waite. vol. 13. Fol. 202. (1546)
7. Ibid. Will of Richard Dawson. Vol. 28. 857. d. Jan. 26. 1602. Will of Marie Dawson. d. 1614.
8. Borthwick. Wills of Heworth Residents.
9. Ibid. Will of William Thwenge. d. 1700. Will of Martha Clapham. d. 1632. Fol. 41. 913.
10. H. Aveling. Northern Catholics. G. Chapman. London. (1966)pp 245- 247. 254-5. 278-79. 346-7.
11. Y.A.S. Claremont Leeds. A. Stewart *Sir Thomas Gascoige or The Yorkshire Plot.* London (1880) pp. 145-50.
12. M. M. Littlehales. Mary Ward – A Woman For All Seasons. Catholic Truth Society. London. (1974)
13. P. Wenham. The Great and Close Seige of York. pp. 113. 114.
14. Osbaldwick History Group. Osbaldwick – A Suburban Village. York Smith. (1980)pp. 33. 34.

CHAPTER III
MESSUAGES AND MANOR HOUSES

Eighteenth Century Landowners

By the middle of the 18th century, because more records such as parish records, church terriers and deeds are available, more place names and names of more Heworth inhabitants appear. The Dawson family had established themselves in Heworth by the late 16th century and owned quite a lot of land and houses in the village. They also leased from the Crown, Heworth Grange, a farmhouse that stood where now a Victorian built Heworth Grange stands, on Heworth Green, just past Villa Grove. William Dawson, mortgaged some of his land in Heworth Village to the Thwenge family "A Capital messuage with five oxgangs of land, one garth late in the tenure of Christopher Peckett now Richard Darnwater. Two cottages or grounds where cottages did stand, late in tenure of Thomas Burton, then in occupation of Margaret Mason and another close called Marston Close adjoining Tang Hall Lane".[1] In 1789, the Rev. Dawson of Calverstone near Shipton sold his Heworth Grange property. "One farmhouse, barn, stable and ten closes of arable meadow and pasture and an extensive brick, tile and pottery manufactory". An advertisement had appeared in the York Courant in October 1779, advertising this property for let or lease. "Heworth Grange Farm near Monk Bridge, together with yards well accustomed for making bricks, tiles and pots".[2]

The Dawson family had also mortgaged some of their Heworth village property at the bottom end of the village in 1736 to William Gossip. "A messuage, one barn, one garth, formerly in the possession of William Britton. One close called Westlands, one close lying east of the village between the Glebelands of the Rector of St. Cuthberts and one close of Hannah Manklins, then Michael Ellis, which opens northwards into the Hemplands and one little house with a small garth".[3] Land that is now allotments off Hempland Lane and over the now Ashley Park estate to Bad Bargain Lane, was sold to Soloman Wilkinson, butcher, in 1786. "Peter Challenor, devisee of Hannah Murgatroyd, heir of Richard Manklin, to Soloman Wilkinson. Two closes called Silver Pools, adjacent on a lane leading to Osbaldwick on the south and Swath Moor Close on the north and lands of Peter Johnson on the west. Also Foss Butts and two little closes called Little Parson Croft and Great Parson Croft". Fields near Cow Moor Bridge down Stockton Lane were called the Lady Closes. Another field called Sugar Hills was in the possession of William Todd, who also owned eighteen acres of Broadfields. In 1743, John Williamson held, "Two closes next to Cow Moor Lane, part of Broadfields, then called Jobson Closes".[4]

Eighteenth Century Inhabitants

Some of the records for this period, such as deeds of land and church records, give not only the names of landowners, but names of the tenants. From these we can learn some of the names of the farmers in Heworth and find out about their occupations in Georgian Times. From a St. Saviour's Church Assessment 1763, we see the names, Mr. Henry Jubb, Joseph Priestley, Mr. J. Wright, J. Harper, Jonathan Crooks, Thomas Bond and Ben Murgatroyd.[5]

Peter Johnson, Recorder of York in the 18th century, acquired the land in Heworth Village owned by the Agars in 1734 and the Kilvingtons in 1736. Robert Johnson Eden, the heir of Peter Johnson, sold most of this land in 1812-13. From a notice of this sale we see the names of George Richardson and John Atkinson, oatshellers, John Wilkinson, Benjamin Stoker, William Sturdy, yeomen. Thomas Todd and Peter Theakstone butchers and Mr. Samuel Ella and Mr. F. Pulleyn, farmers.[6] Most of these farmers lived in the Village street. The oldest houses and cottages were at the bottom end of the village, just past the present day Walnut Tree public house and near the old Britannia Inn. In 1779, Henry Batty and Margaret, daughter of William Hill, sold to Solomen Wilkinson, " A newly built dwelling house with a stable standing on a pice of ground whereon a building called an Ealing formerly stood. Also a newly erected house in Pale Garth, part of two houses formerly joined together, but standing in two separate parishes". These houses could well be the old Britannia Inn and adjoining house, once called Trentholme.

In 1811, John and Catherine Wilkinson lived in a farmhouse at the bottom end of the village. It had been built on the site of an even older house. (All that newly built house with outbuildings, wherein John Wilkinson now dwells, with the garden bounded by a new wall. Also all that tenement, formerly a granary or barn, in the occupation of W. Robinson, which was erected on the site of a stable to a old cottage, converted into a dwelling house.)

Walnut Tree villa was not built until the late 1850's. It doesn't appear on the 1852 Ordnance Survey map. However, that area was known as Walnut Tree Garth on old deeds and the cottages, adjoining Hildreth House, were probably built in the 1820's. " A dwelling house and tenements and other buildings newly erected by G. Richardson in Walnut Tree Garth, or Front Garth, adjoining the garden of John Wilkinson on the east and garth and premises sold by Robert Johnson Eden to William Sturdy on the west.[7]

William Sturdy lived in Yew Lodge, which is probably an 18th century house. Many of the oldest houses that are still standing today were built on the sites of even older houses.

Heworth Cottage

This was the name given to the large 17th century house that stood until 1937, in large grounds, opposite the chapel in Heworth village. The edge of the grounds surrounded by high walls and many tall trees faced Heworth village on one side and Tang Hall Lane, now Melrosegate, opposite Heworth church and the Vicarage. The land was originally owned by the Dawsons, then Richard Kilvington and bought by Peter Johnson in the 18th century. In 1748, it was sold to Thomas Bond, a stage coach proprietor. "Peter Johnson to Thomas Bond stage coachman, all that capital messuage or mansion house with barns etc". [8] Thomas Bond died in 1795 and left his property to his spinster daughter Ann Bond, who on her death, left it to her friend Ann Moore, who had shared the same religious views.

Miss Moore was the daughter of a friend of the Gray family of Gray's Court in York. She had become a family nuisance by growing too religious and prior to her inheritance, had been found a situation as a governess to Mrs. Gray's sister in Derby. However, on becoming a heiress, she was brought back from banishment to her circle of religious friends and independence. She married the Rev. Jocelyn Willey, Curate of St. Cuthberts in 1825. [9] They had the large house, Heworth Hall built in the grounds of Heworth Cottage about 1830. The only two children of Jocelyn and Ann died in infancy, Lucy aged 3 years and Harriet a baby. Ann died in 1838 at the early age of 40 years. [10]

Heworth Cottage, demolished 1938. The last occupants were the Barton family, confectioners and caterers.   (*Courtesy of J Murphy*)

In the 1840's, Charles Alfred Thisleton, Secretary to the Archbishop of York, occupied Heworth Cottage. His first wife Elizabeth died in 1852. In 1847 one of his sons Alex Cockburn Thisleton had died at the early age of 27 years. His eldest daughter, widow of the Rev. Charles Payton, married George Leeman in 1863.[11]

From the 1880's to the 1920's the Kitching family lived at the Cottage. Dr. John Kitching was the medical supervisor of the Retreat and a member of the York Board of Guardians. He died in 1924.[12] The last occupants of the Cottage were the Barton family, who had a catering and confectionery business in York. The house disappeared about 1937. Mr. H. Williamson, builder, who lived on Heworth Green, built new houses, forming part of Heworth Hall Drive, in the grounds.[13]

Heworth Hall

Heworth Hall, built in 1830, was perhaps the largest of the villas that sprang up in Heworth after the Enclosure Awards of the early 19th century. It was built in a classical style. It had eleven bedrooms; two well fitted bathrooms, three fine reception rooms and servants' hall and two staircases. Lawns, flower gardens and tennis courts and stabling for nine horses, surrounded the house.[14] After the death of Ann Willey in 1838, Lucy Willey, Jocelyn's mother lived at the Hall. Jocelyn married again in 1841, Francis (Fanny), second daughter of the Rev. William Carus Wilson. The Willeys endowed Bilton Street School in Layerthorpe and wanted to have a church built in Heworth. Jocelyn Willey had died before Heworth Church was actually built. His widow wanted it to be a memorial to her husband. Although Mrs. Willey had married again, to Sir Trevor Wheler of Leamington and moved away from the area, she did not forget Heworth. Sir Trevor himself laid the foundation stone, but alas was also dead by the day of the Consecration.[15]

The grounds of Heworth Hall, which fronted Melrosegate and Tang Hall Lane, were surrounded in the 1930's by a high wall. Mrs. Sharpe remembered the high walls surrounding the Hall when she was a girl. The gardener, she recalled, would throw apples over the walls for the school children.[16]

Lady Milbank lived there in late Victorian times and Thomas Brogden, brewer and wine and spirit merchant, lived there at the turn of the century. In 1928, the house and twelve acres of building ground were sold by auction. Some semi- detached houses, built by Sherry, Temple and Caffrey, builders, now forming part of Walney Road and Heworth Hall Drive, were built before the house was demolished in 1934.[17]

Heworth Hall, demolished 1934. Houses were built in the grounds before demolition.
(Courtesy of J Murphy)

Enclosures

There was a first attempt at the Enclosure of Heworth Moor in 1776 but the Moor was not actually enclosed until 1822, when awards of land were made to holders of ancient messuages (houses) in Heworth. Most of the large villas on Heworth Green were built at this time and new housing began in the Mill Lane, East Parade area, still called Heworth Moor until the 1860's. In 1817, the 1/2 year grounds (lands that were used for grazing after the crops were taken), had been replaced by Monk Stray owned by the freemen of Monk Ward[18]

The New Manor House

The New Manor House, which still stands next to Monk Stray at the beginning of Monk Avenue, was built in the 1820's for William Bilton Hornby, shoemaker, of Blake Street. He was Lord of the Manor of Heworth in 1850 and principal landowner. He was the last Governor of the Cordwainer's company and on its dissolution in 1808, presented the Mazer bowl to the Dean and Chapter. It had been given to Mr. Hornby as a testimony by the Cordwainer's company. Mr. Hornby had shops in Harrogate and Scarborough. He also loved entertaining and music. It was said that he once had purchased an organ which cost him upwards of one hundred guineas. When he was Sheriff of York he was known to give lavish dinners at the Assembly Rooms. On one such occasion he invited some of the greatest families of York and Yorkshire to a big dinner and Ball. The officers of the Inniskilling Dragoons and their band were to be there. He also arranged for his apprentices to sing at the Ball. However, most of the apprentices had been busy removing several bottles of brandy from the cellars and spent the evening carusing and womanising. When they eventually arrived back to Mr. Hornby's house they found they had been locked out.[19]

Mr. Hornby's son, the Rev. Robert William Bilton Hornby, was born at the Manor House in 1821. In later life he lived at Clifton Garth, Clifton.[20] In 1860, the house was described as having large basement kitchens. The dining rooms and library were on the first floor and drawing rooms and bedrooms on the second and third floors. A wooden balcony which overlooked the Stray was accessible from the long Georgian windows of the second floor rooms. The old balcony has now been replaced by a modern structure. There was also a vinery, gardens, stables, cottage and a coach house adjoining.[21]

The house just further along Stockton Lane, also with a balcony, was called Belle Vue Cottage and was built about the same time. The occupier in 1830 was Mr. John Scott. Land behind this cottage and part of the Manor House estate was acquired by the Centenary Chapel in the 1930's and was used as tennis courts.[22]

The house, Rose Villa, No. 32 Stockton Lane, originally just one house and occupied in the 1850's by Mr. William Briggs was probably built after the Enclosure of Heworth Moor in the 1820's. "A newly built house with small stable, gig house, greenhouse, outbuildings, garden and paddock, bounded by Stockton Lane on the north, lands of W. Sturdy on the south and on the west J. Empson".[23] On the 1850's Ordnance Survey map it was known as Heworth Villa. In the 1870's Mr. William Stowe Sharp lived there and the Challengers in the 1930's The Author remembers the house in the 1940's. It had large gardens full of snowdrops. She remembers alterations being made to the house whilst she was stopping with her friend, Cynthia Stirk, who lived in the house next door. Her father owned Stirk's Furnishing Stores in Layerthorpe. Chestnut trees, some which are still there, fringed the edges of the garden along Stockton Lane. The Stead family built a modern bungalow in the gardens in the 1960's.[24]

The house, Chestnut Grove, and its grounds that ran up to Stockton Lane and Heworth Road corner was built about 1830. The Cobb family, described as paper manufacturers, were living here in 1840. It later became known as The Pleasaunce, a private mental asylum, run by Dr. Leonard D. H. Baugh. It closed in the early 1930s and more houses in Seymour Grove were built along Stockton Lane and around the corner into Heworth Road which had formed part of the asylum's grounds.[25]

Heworth Green Villas

The large villas on Heworth Green were built after the Enclosure of Heworth Moor in the 1820's. Most feature in the Royal Commission Book on houses worth preserving. The Limes, originally called Terrace Cottage, was built for Mr. Richard Hornby around this time. It was a was a detached three bay villa, white brick with a stone plinth. The occupiers in the early part of this century were the Foster-Todds. In the 1950's The Limes became a hostel for St. John's College, now the College of Ripon and St. John.

By the 1830's there was also No. 110, Heworth Green Villa, and a detached three bay villa called Heworth Green Cottage. On the 1852 ordnance survey map No. 108 Heworth Cottage was attached to an older 19th Century house. Cupola House was also built around this time. These villas were originally called Heworth Place, later Scarborough Parade. The occupants in the 1840's were Mr. William Dibb, a clerk, Captain Anthony Graves and Mr. Henry Cobb. The small parade of houses past these big villas up to Mill Lane corner were built about 1830-1850. Some of the occupants then were Mr. Henry Bellerby, Mr. Benjamin Smallpage, Mr. James Hodgson, surgeon at Eastern Villa and Mr. Thomas Ridley at Clifton House.[26]

Mr. John Donaldson lived along Eastern Terrace in the 1840's, possibly at the house that is now Eastern Villa. In 1852, after his death, the house was sold. It was described as a cottage, with outbuildings and gardens, two sitting rooms, back kitchens and pantry, four bedrooms and lumber-room.[27] The public house, the Shoulder of Mutton had been built by the 1830's, In 1840 the landlord was Mr. John Poulter. This public house was then at no. 74 and it did not move to its present position until the 1950's.

Heworth Grange estate, where now Dodsworth Avenue and Pottery Lane are was land that was once granted to St. Mary's Abbey, then leased by St. Leonard's Hospital. After the Dissolution, the Crown acquired this land but it was leased by the Dawson family until 1779. Heworth Grange was a Victorian house built on the site of an older Norman farmhouse. It still has the crest of Victoria and Albert and was occupied in the 1870's by Mr. Henry Moiser, land agent and surveyor for Oxford University and large scale estate owners.[28]

Crown Cottage

Crown Cottage or Queens Villa was a large house that once stood near the Monk Bridge end of Heworth Green. It was built in the 1830's, for the Rev. John Acaster, Vicar of St. Helens. The land on which it was built on was leased from the Crown. It was described in 1852 as having dining rooms, drawing rooms and a kitchen on the first floor. Five best lodging rooms, dressing rooms and servants rooms above. There was an excellent larder, wine and beer cellar and water closet. There were stables, coach house, piggeries and cowhouse. There were also pleasure grounds, gardens, and a plantation surrounding the property which ran down to the River Foss.[29] In the 1890's the Dove family lived here. In the 1920, s it was renamed Dalguise House and turned into flats. The house was demolished in the 1930;s and the new housing development, Dalguise Grove and houses on Heworth Green were built.

The Woodman Inn

On the opposite side of Heworth Green, where now the Gas Works car park stands near the old Monk Bridge, was the Woodman Inn. William Fawdington was the landlord in the 1850's. He was also a timber merchant. A lane that leads from this area to Layerthorpe, at the side of the gas works, was called Fawdington lane, possibly named after this gentleman. When Monk Bridge was rebuilt in the 1920's, this Inn was demolished. The remains of a medieval hospital were found under the foundations of this building.[30]

Monk Bridge before alterations in the 1920's. On the left is the old Woodman Inn and on the right the wall surrounding the grounds of Dalguise House (formerly Crown Cottage).   *(Courtesy of City of York Library)*

The Glen

The Glen, or Glen Heworth, as it was originally known was built for Dr. Simpson in the 1830's. It stood down Bull Lane, south of East Parade and the grounds extended over the now Glen Park. In 1857, Miss Barbara Lawson lived here. In the 1860's, William Leak, a draper and founder of the famous department store, Leak and Thorp had moved to the Glen. He altered the house, doubled its size and added more bedrooms, which he leased to his shop assistants. Some of his land, which now is part of Glen Park, was sold to York Corporation before the 1st World War.

Glen Park was officially opened in 1915. Dr Lythe lived at the Glen between the wars. In the 1950's the house became a residential council home and day nursery but was pulled down in the 1960's. An Old People's Home, Glen Lodge, now occupies this site.[31]

The Tang Hall

The name Tang means the area or pond where two becks meet. The Tang Hall was the name given to the house that once stood in an area between Fourth Avenue and Tang Hall Lane. It had originally been a medieval farmhouse. The Tang Hall area that stretched from Bull Lane to the Hull Road was once just fields and pasture grounds owned by the Prebend of Fridaythorpe. At the end of the 15th century the City succeeded in establishing a right to pasture their cows on the land and Tang Hall Fields become one of the City's pasture grounds after 1525, although it was actually owned by the Ecclesiastical Commissioners from 1490-1830.[32] In the 18th century there are records of leases of the house and fields. In 1767, a capital messuage was leased to Bernard Ackroyd, brewer and in 1781 the dwelling house called Tang Hall and various closes to Ralph Bean, innkeeper. In the time of bad plagues in York in the 16th century the cows were taken off Tang Hall Fields. Plague victims were placed in plague lodges erected on these fields.[33]

In the 1830's, James Barber, a York silversmith and lord of the Manor of Osbaldwick, bought the Tang Hall estate for £10,000. He altered the house and made it into a Victorian manor house. He used his land surrounding the house to pasture the horses for his famous coaching business at the Black Swan in Coney Street.[34]

In the 1880's, Captain Edward Charles Starkey and Lady Evelyne Starkey lived at this house. Captain Starkey died in 1906 and there is a tablet to his memory in Heworth church. Lady Starkey lived alone at this house after his death. It was rumoured that she became rather eccentric in her later years and it was said she shot nails and grapeshot at trespassers on her land. Her brothers had been early Australian pioneers and the ghost of one of her brothers was said to live in the coach house at the Tang Hall.[35] Lady Starkey was also known to take people on jaunts around Buttercrambe Woods in her pony trap for half a crown. After her death in 1925, her estate was put up for sale and bought by York Corporation, who then built up the Tang Hall and Melrosegate areas. One road was subsequently named Starkey Crescent after its previous owner. The Tang

Hall council estate was begun in the 1920's and re-housed people from the Layerthorpe and Walmgate areas. The Tang Hall became a public house in the 1930's, demolished sadly in the 1970's and a new public house was built just off Fourth Avenue.[36]

This was the home of the Starkey family in the early part of the 20th Century. In the 1930's it became Tang Hall Hotel. It was demolished in the late 1970's.

(Courtesy of City of York Library)

Tang Hall Bridge Circa 1900.

Chapter III. Notes and References

1 Borthwick. *Will of William Dawson*. fol. 67. (1681).
2. Y.R.L. *York Courant*. 19. Oct. (1779). (1789).
3. Borthwick. *Deeds*. (1736). (1786). (1743).
4. Y.R.L. *York Courant*. (1796). Sale of Manor of Heworth. N.R. Register of Deeds. AM 367 473
5. Borthwick. *St. Saviour's Church Assessment*. (1763).
6. Sale of P. Johnson's Lands sold by R. J. Eden Johnson. (1812-13).
7. N.R.R.O. *Deeds* B.O. 247 370 (1779) D. M. 481. 569. (1811). E.X. 304. 284.(1823)
8. N.R.R. *Deeds*. S111/142. (1748). J. Kilvington. mortgages Messuage called Pond Garth. (1736). Debt purchased by Johnson. Sold to T. Bond.
9. Y.R.L. Gray. E. *Papers and Diaries of a York Family*. (1764-1839). (London) 1927. pp 240/41.
10. Borthwick. PRY/Cu. *Deaths*. (1835-1840).
11. Y.R.L. Newspaper Index. *A. Thisleton*. Obit. Y. G. 18. 12. (1847).
12. Ibid. John Kitching. Obit. Y. G. 5. 4. (1924).
13. Y.R.L. *Kelly's Directories Ltd*. York. (1930). Y. C. C. Minutes. (1960).
14. Y.R.L. *Sale of Heworth Hall*. 25. Oct. (1928).
15. Borthwick. PRY/CU. *Deaths*. (1838). PRY/ST. SAV. 18. Marriages. (1841)
16. Information supplied by Mrs. A. Sharpe, 25 Heworth Road.
17. Kelly's. 1850-1890. Y.C.C. *Minutes*. (1930).
18. Borthwick. *Heworth Enclosure Award*. (1822).
19. Y.R.L. J. Shepherd. *Reflections and Observations on Occurrences in a Private Life*. Y.920 (pamphlet)
20. Y.R.L. Newspaper Index. *William Bilton Hornby*.
21. *Y. Gazette*. 27.7. 1861.
22. Information supplied by Miss K. Hayes, 45 Forest Grove.
23. N.R.R.O. *Deeds*. F.N. 310. 315.
24. Information supplied by Mrs. A. Appleton (née Reeder), 18 Whitby Drive. *Kelly's* (1930's).
25. Y. Gazette. *Dr. Baugh*. Obit. 9. 5. (1933).
26. Royal Commission on Historical Monuments. *City of York*. Vol 1V. . London. (1975) p26. *Kelly's*. 1850.
27. *Y. Gazette*. 6. 11. 1852.
28. *Kelly's*. (1850-1870) Y.A.R.S. *Yorkshire Charters* vol.11 p 370.
29. *Y. Gazette*. 5. 8. 1854.
30. Y.C.C. *Minutes*. 1920's. & Raine. A. *Medieval York*. p. 284.
31. Waterson, E. and Meadows. P. *Lost Houses of York and the North Riding*. Jill Raines (1990). P. 66.
32. Tillot. P.(ed). V.C.H. *The City of York*. p.500.
33. Y.C.A. E101 210 (1767) E101.282.(1781).
34. Tillot. (ed). op cit 32. P. 501.
35. Tanghall Library. Fr. Armand Carré. Middlesborough.(1982) *Notes on Tang Hall and St. Aelred's Church*.
36. Information. Mr. Bridge. 20 First Ave. Y.C.C.M. (1920-1930). (1970s).

CHAPTER IV
VICTORIAN HEWORTH

By the time the reign of Victoria had begun, Heworth was much more built up. There were houses down Heworth Road, East Parade, Mill Lane and Heworth Green. The cottages in Danby Terrace, opposite the church had been built by the 1850's. Edinboro Cottage, Rose Cottage, Montrose Villa and South View are all mentioned in the 1860's directories. Most of the houses and cottages along East Parade, opposite the Glen Gardens, down to Mill lane corner were occupied by the 1850's.[1] The first houses in First and Second Avenue were started in the 1890's built by Wray builders. This land was previously owned by the Church and sold in 1894.[2]

What sort of people lived in these houses? They seem to have had a variety of occupations. There were telegraphists, salesmen and commercial travellers, photographers, rent collectors, schoolmasters, shopkeepers and a straw hat dealer.[3]

The Horse Bus travelling along East Parade towards the terminus at Wesley House next to the chapel.circa 1900. *(Courtesy of P. Wheatley)*

21

A Victorian Jockey

In 1876, Simon Templeman, a top class Victorian jockey, came to live in East Parade. He had won the Derby three times, also the Oaks, the St. Ledger and the Ebor Handicap. During the course of his career he enjoyed the patronage of Baron Rothschild, Lord Derby and Lord Chesterfield. He married a York girl. He retired from racing in the late 1850's to breed horses on his farm at Burnby near Pocklington. He died in 1884 and is buried in York Cemetery.[4]

Heworth Road

The row of houses and cottages on Heworth Road just past Dale's Lane, was called Heworth Terrace in the 1850's. The first house, now the laundrette and video shop, was called Prospect House then and occupied by Mr. Walker, builder. Dale's Lane was only a narrow track that led to Paradise Cottage and fields owned by Mr. Dale in the 1850's and Mr. Pulleyn in the 1870's. Heworth Church School was built by 1873 and the row of cottages near the school ended at the Police Station.[5] The Nag's Head public house was mentioned in a Deed of 1830, then called a brew house.[6] The cottages that stand next to it were probably built in the 1830's also. These were called Bennett's Row then and the small cottages that once stood in a yard behind the Nag's Head, Bennett's Yard. The people who lived in these cottages were mostly labourers, gardeners, grooms, cowkeepers and warehousemen.

Heworth Road showing the school, shop and N.R. Police station. Circa 1900.

(W. Hayes)

22

In the 1870's Mr. Garton Horsley had a shop and Post Office in Heworth Road, Mr. Beaumont was a coal dealer and William Hunter the Superintendent of Police for the North Riding Constabulary.

Heworth Green Villas

The people who lived in the large villas on Heworth Green in the 1850's were mostly middle class. There were solicitors, schoolmasters and ministers. There was a private girl's boarding school run by two sisters from London. By the 1860's, this had removed to Bootham. The terrace of houses which ran from the old Shoulder of Mutton public house to Eastern Terrace was called Scarborough Parade in the 1850's. On the other side of Malton Road were Benjamin Walker, pot and tile manufacturer; Henry Moiser, land agent at the Grange; Mrs. Champney at New Villa, later called Edenheys; Mr. Henry Ware at the Croft and William Dove at Crown Cottage.

Stockton Lane

In the 1850's, few houses occupied Stockton Lane. There was the New Manor House, Bellevue Cottage and a few farmhouses past Monk Stray. On the other side of Stockton Lane, was the big house, Chestnut Grove. The grounds of this house extended up to the corner of Stockton Lane and Heworth Road. Mr. Briggs was living at Rose Villa and Mr. Simpson had his market garden where Forest Way is now. Further along Stockton Lane there were a few more farms. Mr. Collinson was at Appletree Farm and Mr. Bean, market gardener at Sugar Hill's Farm. W. Pratt, R. Theakstone, J. Wrigglesworth and William Ridsdell were farmers along Malton Road. Mr. Butler was a hay and straw merchant, Mr. Elliker was at the Hopgrove Inn and Mr. William Wilberforce, a farmer and chicory grower.[7]

Chestnut House

This house, which still stands at the end of Heworth Village, Walnut Tree side, was once in Georgian and early Victorian times, a private mental home called Heworth Retreat. It was described as having spacious and cheerful rooms, well ventilated, with grounds adapted for exercise and recreation of patients. An extract from the Commissioners report on Asylums in 1840, stated that, "Heworth Retreat was clean and well ventilated. No patients were under restraint, books and needlework was supplied to females and all were treated kindly".[8]

In the 1870's, this house was sold as a private residence, then called Chestnut House. A large chestnut tree once stood outside this house. Chestnut House was described in 1873 as having ample room for a family, an extensive walled garden, stable, coach house, cow house and outbuildings. It had been in the

The last house on the left was once called Chestnut House, later the name changed to Tranent. This picture shows the large Chestnut tree that stood outside until the 1980's. The gate at the bottom is on Hempland Lane and led into the grounds of St. Cuthbert's Rectory which would be behind the trees. Circa 1900.   *(Courtesy of J. Murphy)*

occupation of George Bell, currier, deceased. Mr. Bell had bought this house in the 1860's, after the mental home closed. His leather works were in Lowther Street in the Groves. Mr. Horsley lived at this house in the 1880's.

Village Houses

In Victorian times more houses and cottages were built in the Village street. The Walnut Tree Villa is mentioned in the directories of 1860, the occupant then was Mr. Joseph Kimber, grocer of Goodramgate and Heworth. His daughter married Mr. John Richard Hill, tanner and currier of St. Saviourgate and James Street. An entry in the York Courant for 1873, stated that a house or messuage was for sale in the Village. It had outbuildings and a productive garden and had formerly been in the occupation of John Scott, now Mr. George Nursaw was the yearly tenant. This would be the house now known as Yew Lodge.

There were also several cottages, newly erected, adjoining the above mentioned house and fronting the town street of Heworth, in the occupation of T. Robinson, W. Pulleyn, E. Ferrand, Mrs. Baldwin and H. Smith. There was another house for sale, next to the cottages, It had a yard, cowhouses, stables and piggeries and grass land adjoining called Ash Tree Garth, then occupied by Mr.

W. Newbold, cowkeeper. There was also a cottage in the yard in the occupation of T. Kettlewell, labourer and three newly erected cottages fronting the street from Heworth to York in the respective occupations of J. Dunford, A. Simpson and G. Windruss and a paddock behind in the occupation of H. Wilson, joiner.[9] The house would probably be Beech House and the cottages mentioned, Spring Cottages. Mr. Henry Wilson lived at the house now called Hildreth House. In 1873, he bought the land near Heworth Chapel and built the terrace of houses just before the chapel, which later became shops.[10] The row of houses, just past the chapel, called Elm Terrace in 1890, were probably built in the 1870's. The Britannia Inn, now a private house, no.s 70 & 72, was first licensed in 1806.[11] In 1863 it was put up for sale, described as "A brew house with large yard and garden, previously occupied by Mrs. Jane Britton, with a cottage, stable and loose box".[12]

Heworth Church of England School

Heworth Voluntary Primary School, as it was originally called, was opened in 1873 in a building on Heworth Road erected with the aid of a Government grant. The fees were 2d and 3d for boys, 2d, 3d, and 4d for girls and 1d and 2d for infants. In 1877 the average attendance was 140. In 1910 there were two departments, junior mixed and infants.[13]

Elmfield College

Elmfield College was established in 1864, around the old Elmfield Villa, which had once been the home of Mr. F Hill, on the east side of Malton Road, as a Primitive Methodist boarding school. In 1865 there were ninety two boarders, eight, day pupils and a staff of six and the average yearly fee was £31. In 1906, the school was closed by the Trustees for the Connection because of financial difficulties but re-opened in 1907. A laboratory, workshop and extra classrooms costing £1,500 were added in 1909. In June 1924, the school celebrated its Diamond Jubilee. To record this landmark and to commemorate the Old Boys who fell in the Great War, a new cricket field and pavilion was erected. A fund for these improvements was raised by the Old Boys who owned and managed the college then. The ceremony of laying the first stone of the pavilion was performed on Monday the 9th June. A diamond jubilee dinner, attended by many Old Boys, was held on the Saturday and a special service on the Sunday took place in the John Petty Memorial Chapel.[14]

The school prided itself on the spartan training, which was thought to build up character. Mr. Smith, who was a pupil at the school in the early part of this century, remembered his days at Elmfield. He recalled having to wash in cold water and go for long runs in all weathers. He said that the dormitories were very cold with few bedcovers and little or no home comforts.

ELMFIELD COLLEGE.

W. Hayes
YORK

This was a Primitive Methodist Boarding School. Demolished in the 1930s except the
first house on the right. *(Courtesy of J. Murphy)*

In 1932, the school ran into more financial problems and was closed, many
pupils were transferred to Ashville College at Harrogate. The buildings were
demolished, except for the original house which is still there today, next to the
Stray on Stray Road. New residential housing was built in the grounds around
about 1935.[15]

Brickworks and Potteries

There are mentions of brickworks and potteries in Heworth since Georgian
and early Victorian times. Paul Batty was advertising his yard for sale in 1770.
This was situated near Heworth Grange, where bricks, tiles and pottery could
be manufactured. In 1790 John Bollans advertised in the York Herald that he
had taken the pottery at Mr. Samuel Ella's Brick and Tile yard, Heworth Grange,
lately occupied by Mrs. Wedgewood. In the early part of the 18th century John
Wedgewood had moved his pottery from Yearsley, near Coxwold to Heworth
Moor. After his death his widow ran the business. There appears to have been
at least two potteries and a brickfield on Heworth Moor, off Pottery Lane, now
part of the Heworth Golf course. A small narrow gauge railway was built on
the Moor to transport the clay and bricks to the yards. Robert Bewlay and later
Benjamin Walker seemed to have been brickmakers in this area in Victorian
times and Mr. Martin in the early years of this century. There was another
brickyard and kilns at the back of the houses now called Elmfield Terrace to the
east of Malton Road. A narrow track along Willow Grove led to Eden House, and

cottages and brick kilns called Eden Place. Robert Gibson, John Freeman and John Webster seemed to have been the brickmakers and potters associated with these works. These brickworks were in use until the 1920's and there are still brickponds and an old pump house in that area.[16]

In the 1840's, the growth of railways, canals and bridges opened the way for a building boom, of which bricks played a major part. There were many small family brickworks in Victorian times. Brickmakers were notorious for being rowdy and troublesome. They often had a long break at dinnertime in the hottest part of the day and many went for a drink then. However they were supposed to start work again at 4pm but some were too drunk to restart. Children were employed in brickworks, often working long hours and doing hot and dangerous jobs. In 1870 an act was passed to regulate child and female labour in brickworks. At the end of the Victorian period, there was a move from the small family firms to larger scale brick companies.[17]

The Limes

By the 1890's, more prominent Victorian families had come to live in Heworth. On Heworth Green in 1870, Mr. Richard Feltoe was living at The Limes. He had married Miss Francis Hornby, daughter of Richard Hornby. In 1894 the house was put up for auction. It was described then as a villa residence with orchard, gardens, shrubberies, vinery, cucumber pits, coach house and stables, workshop, piggery and poultry houses. The gardens were laid out with choice shrubs and fruit trees and surrounded by a belt of Lime trees. The basements of the house contained cellars for beer, wine and coal. On the ground floor there was a drawing room with french windows, dining room with a large bay window, breakfast room or study and two good kitchens. There were four bedrooms and dressing rooms on the first floor. There was also a bathroom and lavatory, hot and cold water and servants' rooms. The estate also contained five cottages in Heworth Road and Rose Cottage near the junction of East Parade, which had coach house and stables and was occupied then by a Mr. Malyon.[18]

Heworth Villas

Mr. Coton lived at Cupola House and the Bland family at Heworth Villa in later Victorian times. Mr. Joseph Mann lived at Eastern Villa. He was a City Councillor and had a carriage factory and show rooms in Monkgate. Just past the old Shoulder of Mutton, were two houses, near the entrance to Cinder Lane, Sutherland House and The lodge. Mr. J. C. Walker, ironmonger, lived at Sutherland House and Mr. W. Sharpe, a pawnbroker, who had his shop at the end of St. Saviourgate, lived at The Lodge.[19]

Clifton House

The big house, which stands on the other side of Cinder Lane, now the new Shoulder of Mutton, was called Clifton House in the 1890's and occupied by a Mr. H. Buckton. There were gardens fronting Heworth Green and behind the house a long lawn, kitchen garden and orchards stretched down the side of Cinder Lane to East Parade, an area of 4,850 sq. yards. This house became known as Heworth Hyrst at the turn of the century, occupied by the Lyth family. A house and farm building stood at the end of Wood Street fronting Cinder Lane.[20]

Miss Edith Milner

At Heworth Moor House, originally called The Cottage, lived Miss Edith Milner. She was the eldest daughter of Sir William and Lady Milner of Nun Appleton. She was a well known leader of county society and the foundress of the Milner Habitation of the Primrose League. This was a society, which, in 1883, was established to support the Conservative party. Her house was said to be a constant resort of fashionable society and she entertained may important Victorian gentry including Lord Charles Beresford and Sir Frederick Milner M.P., a near relative. She served on many local committees and held very definite views and was often at loggerheads with the authorities. She was a frequent letter writer to the local newspapers. During the 1st World War she held garden fetes and bazaars to raise money for the armed forces.[21] Mrs. Poole remembered going to tea and also sewing shirts for the 1st World War soldiers at her house.[22] Miss Milner had abundant energy and it was said, in her latter years, when she became sleepy after lunch or in the evening, she would play cards until the tired feeling receded. She died in 1921.[23]

Heworth Green

Just past Eastern Terrace lived Alfred Gibbons, F.S.A., a well known genealogist. Further along Heworth Green, near the Mill Lane turning, lived Mr. Henry Bellerby and Mr. Benjamin Smallpage, the latter being one of the founders of the well-known house furnishers, Hunter and Smallpage. Mr. Hayes lived at Westfield House and Mrs. Hodgson at St. Maurice House. On the other side of Heworth Green, where Dodsworth Avenue is now, the N.E. Railway Company had established their laundry in 1895. The manageress then was Mrs. S. Smith. Mr. Moiser was still at Heworth Grange, Mrs. Champney, New Villa, Mr. Dove, Crown Cottage and Mrs. Craven at Heworth Croft.[24]

The Dove family, ironmongers, had first opened their shop in Pavement in 1803, having purchased the ironmongery stock of Mr. R. Gibson. They opened a shop in Piccadilly in 1931 and were there until 1962. In Victorian times this family lived at Crown Cottage and their son married into the Craven family. Mr. Fawdington, horse dealer was at the end of Heworth Green, near the bridge. His son was a veterinary surgeon in the early 1900's.[25]

There were cottages in Mill Lane in Victorian times. The big house, now part of London's newsagents was built around 1870, then called Millington House. The gardens extended up to Layerthorpe Railway Bridge.

The Foster family had taken over the provisions shop at the end of East Parade opposite Millington House by 1890. This family was there until the 1950's.[26]

Sister Wilson's Homes

Sister Wilson's Homes were founded by Mary Wilson in 1885 for 10 poor women over 60. They comprised of two adjoining brick dwelling houses in East Parade and two cottages in Mill Lane. In 1946 the inmates each received a pension of 4s a week but it was reported then that there was dampness in some of the dwellings and a demolition order was placed on them in 1957.[27]

Heworth Village

In late Victorian times Mrs. Sarah Hudson lived at Newton House, which was the first house past the entrance to Dale's Lane. Now it is a Spar shop. Mrs. Hudson was a costumer and mantle maker. Miss Mary Bingham lived at the next house, then called Trinity House, now it is a delicatessen and Mr. Kidd lived at Oak House, now the chemist shop.

Mr. William Bell lived at Wesley House next to the chapel (this house was demolished in 1967 for chapel extensions). He was described as a paperhanger and postmaster in 1890. This house was also the terminus for the Heworth horse bus from York. The row of houses up to Yew Lodge was called Elm Crescent in these times.

Mr. Hagyard, market gardener was living in one of these in 1895 and Mr. Enoch John Stanhope at Yew Lodge. There were people living in Harrison Street and Clarke's Terrace by 1900.[28] Mrs. Dennis had her laundry in the cottage behind Spring Cottages where the White House is now. In the council minutes for 1901, there are complaints about keeping pigs behind these cottages. Sanitary notices, to repair defective drains, were also served on the owners of these cottages. There were also complaints about defective drains at Newton House and Heworth Hall at this time. In 1880, William Horsley was living at Chestnut House, and Henry Wilson, joiner and builder at Hildreth House next door, now a dental practice, formerly Sorrell's builders. Mr. Moorfoot, farmer, lived at the Old Manor House, which was opposite the Walnut Tree, and the Halliwell family resided at Trentholme, the large house adjoining the Britannia Inn.

Heworth Road

In Heworth Road, Mrs. Bikerdike lived at Rose Cottage, Mr. Glover was at his shop near the school and Mr. Gibb, general manager of the N.E. Railway Co.

lived near the Police Station. By the last years of Queen Victoria, the Herbert family had taken over the Nag's Head Public House.[30]

Stockton Lane

By 1900, there were a few more houses in Stockton Lane, although the majority of the houses were not built until the 1920's and 30's. The big house, Chestnut Grove, had changed its name to the Pleasaunce, and had become a private mental home. Mr. William Stowe Sharpe lived at Rose Villa. Mr. Simpson's nurseries extended over what is now Forest Way up to Dale's Lane. The rows of houses, with fancy Victorian architecture, between Chestnut and Lime, opposite the New Manor House, were built around 1900. The De Burgh family built these, the last one aptly named Turret House, later called De Burgh House. The first houses in Whitby Avenue were built by Mr. Walker of York and Whitby in the 1890's.[31]

Mrs. Beaumont's Memories

Mrs. Beaumont recalled that she was born in the first house, just past the end of Whitby Avenue, then called Horton Cottage, in the early years of this century. Her father, Mr. Alfred Kay, a grocer and chapel organist, had bought it at a knocked down price as he had said the builder had gone bankrupt. She remembered her childhood in that area. She recalled that Whitby Avenue was always full of potholes. She picked wild flowers in the fields just past the end of Whitby Avenue, then the road only went as far as the old houses and terminated at a gate. She remembered her neighbours, the Sharper family, the father was a chemist. She recalled also, the Watson and Herbert families of Stockton Lane and her particular friend, Phyllis Lee, who lived down Whitby Avenue.[32]

Burnholme - A Victorian Country House

The large property which for many years has been the home of Burnholme Social Club, was almost certainly completed for habitation about 1882. The Burnholme Estate was originally owned by Samuel Atkinson of Osbaldwick, who left it all when he died, to his brother and sisters. In 1835, it was owned by Eleanor Atkinson who married George Foster.[33] In the 1880's John Bellerby, owner of St. George's Saw Mills in Walmgate, bought it and it was he who had the house built, designed by William Pentry. John Bellerby was born in 1833 and as well as owning the sawmills was a Director of York Gas Co., Managing Director of York City and County Bank, Director of York Herald Newspaper Co. and Governor of various institutions. He married first, Margaret Graham of Selby, who bore him 10 children but who died in 1873 at the early age of 35. He married again and lived at Burnholme House for about eight years before moving to Fulford, although he probably retained the ownership.

The new occupier was Harry Leetham, a prominent local businessman. He was a corn miller in Hungate, a staunch Methodist and teetotaller and was Vice President of the British Temperance League.

The Census of 1891 records 57 year old Mr. Leetham, his wife Mary and three of their children with four young domestic servants living at Burnholme. In a separate dwelling, now part of Burnholme Mews, a 27-year-old coachman and his wife were living.[34]

Mr. Leetham died at Burnholme in 1896 and after that, his family moved from this house. Mr. Bellerby returned to live at Burnholme for a while.[35]

The gardener with servants from Burnholme House. Housekeeper, Mrs. Collinson (holding child). Circa 1900. *(Courtesy of Mrs. D. Mortimer)*

Mr. Robert Collinson, coachman, outside Burnholme House. It is now a Working Men's Club. Circa 1900. *(Courtesy of Mrs. D. Mortimer)*

Chapter IV. Notes and References.

1. Y.R.L. *York Directories.* (1850-1860)
2. *Sale of Church Lands.* 1894. Supplied by Mrs. F. Shaw, 90 East Parade.
3. *Kelly's. Directories.* (1850-1870)
4. Information supplied by Mr. D. Poole, 19 Penyghent Ave.
5. *Kelly's.* (1850-1870)
6. Y.C.A. *York Deed* 1830.
7. *Kelly's* (1850-1870).
8. *Y. Gazette.* 14.11.1840.
9. Ibid. 3. 5. 1873.
10. Y.C.A. 16.10.1873
11. *Kelly's* 1870-1890. N.Y. Police Licensing Office.
12. *Y. Gazette* 24.9.1863
13. 7. P. M. Tillot.(ed) V.C.H. *The City of York.* (1961) p.448.
14. *Y.E.P.* 7.6.1924.
15. Information. Mr. Smith, Ramsay, Isle of Man.
16. *Y. Courant.* 19.10.1779. Lawrence, M. *Yorkshire Pots and Potteries.*
17. Y.C.A. Garside-Neville, S. *Brickmaking in York in the 19th century.* (1994)
18. Y.R.L. 942. 74/Y. Hew. Deeds. *Sale of The Limes.* 1894.
19. *Kelly's.* 1890-1902.
20. Y.R.L. *Plan of Clifton House.* (1893)
21. Y.R.L. *Cuttings Book.* 1914-1923.
22. Information. Mrs. B. Poole, 6 Horsman Avenue.
23. op cit 21.
24. *Kelly's* (1890-1902)
25. Murray, H. *Pedigrees of York Families.*
26. *Kelly's.* (1850. -1902)
27. V.C.H. p. 426.
28. *Kelly's* (1890-1902)
29. Y.C.A. *York City Council Minutes.* (1890-1902).
30. Op Cit. 28.
31. Information supplied by Mrs. Greear (Late), Hempland Lane.
32. Memories of Mrs. Beaumont. Lamel Beeches, Heslington Lane.
33. Deeds and Information. Mr. W. Maddison, 26 Mill Lane.
34. Information. Mr. D. Poole, 19 Penyghent Avenue.
35. Information. Mrs. D. Mortimer, St. Thomas Close, Osbaldwick.
36. *Y. Gazette.* 1896.

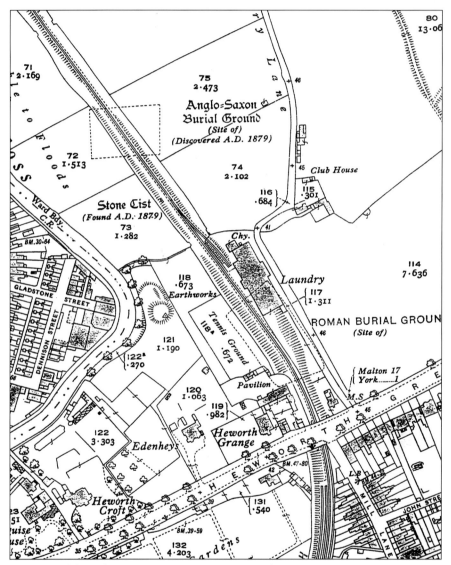

Reproduced from the 1920 OS map. Crown Copyright.

CHAPTER V
THE EARLY YEARS OF THE 20TH CENTURY

Burnholme House

By 1909, the occupier was the Hon. Francis Stanley Jackson who had previously lived at Heworth Hall. A younger son of Lord Allerton of Chapel Allerton, he was a man of enormous and diverse talents. A brilliant cricket all rounder, he played in twenty test matches all against Australia, scoring five centuries and captained England to victory in the 1905 series. He played for his native Yorkshire from 1890-1912, but was often away because of overseas business commitments. He was regarded as the epitome of the "Golden Age of English Cricket". He married Miss Harrison-Broadley, eldest daughter of Mr. & Mrs. Harrison-Broadley of Welton Hall near Hull. Members of the Yorkshire Eleven attended the wedding and the marriage ceremony was performed by the Dean of York. The Hon. Jackson subsequently went into politics being M.P. for Howdenshire 1915-1926, Governor of Bengal, President of both Yorkshire County Cricket Club, and the M.C.C. On the local scene he was the first President of Heworth Golf Club when it formed in 1911. He enlarged Burnholme House, adding a billiard room to the back, decorated with woodcarvings of animals supposedly illustrating the various countries in which he had visited. It is not certain when Jackson vacated Burnholme, but a subsequent owner was Major Tom Preston, whose family seat was Moreby Hall near Stillingfleet.[1]

During the 1st World War, Burnholme House became the headquarters of the 76th squadron R.F.C.; the commanding officer was Major Tom Preston. An aerodrome was situated in Osbaldwick down Murton Way. Major Preston departed in the late 1920's and sold the estate to a consortium of local businessmen, who were to create a short-lived speedway stadium.[2]

Electric Buses

At the beginning of the 1st World War, York Corporation decided to purchase four battery operated buses from the Edison Electric Company, because of the petrol shortage. They were 24 seaters, one man operated and cost £1,172 each. They were housed in a depot in Foss Islands Road, which was equipped with charging boards for the batteries. Battery charging boards were also erected in shelters built at the top of Stockton Lane, now a flower shop, and one at Clifton Green which were the termini for the new service. Pavement was the halfway stage. Many people recalled the electric buses and having to help to push start the vehicles from the bus shelter at the Stockton Lane end. By the end of the war the buses were all worn out and a trolley bus service was introduced. The part of the shelter that housed the battery charging equipment was opened as a tobacconist. This only closed in the 1980's. Now it is a flower shop.[3]

An Electric Bus outside the Stockton Lane shelter. This was used as a battery charging station.
(Courtesy J. Murphy)

Trolley and Motor Buses

The first motor buses purchased by the Corporation arrived in the 1st World War years. Many buses were fitted with gas bags owing to the acute petrol shortage then. On the Leeman Road route these could not be carried in the conventional position on the roof due to the restrictive height of Leeman Road railway bridge. These buses on this route had their gasbags mounted on a trailer, which was drawn behind the bus. Motor buses were introduced into the Heworth route in the 1920's. However it was decided to keep the trolley bus service as well because of operating costs of motor buses. The last trolley bus ran from Heworth in 1936.[4]

Mrs. Poole's Memories

Many of the children who lived in Heworth in these times attended Heworth School. Mrs. Poole, who lived in Layerthorpe, went to this school during the 1st World War. She did not know why her parents had sent her to Heworth, as there already was a good school, Bilton Street School in Layerthorpe. However, her two good friends, Ada Churchyard and Mona Preston went with her. They all used to walk from Layerthorpe, morning and afternoon and also home for lunch. She recalled they once all had identical pink dresses to wear, of which they were very proud. Mr. Barratt was the Headmaster then and was very strict. She remembered him caning some boys for failing to stop in when told to after school. If they had not gone straight home in time to help with the milking, they would have been in trouble also. She recalled some of the teachers then, Miss Craike, Miss Harrison and her brother Mr. Nettleton. She learned sums, spelling, reading, history and geography. She enjoyed sewing, knitting and darning. Friday afternoon between 3pm and 4pm was singing time.[5]

Mr. Bridge's Memories

Mr. Norman Bridge attended Heworth School about the same time as Mrs. Poole. He and his brother Albert had to help milk the cows on their farm, Denmark Cottage, Malton Road. They also had to deliver the milk to their grandmother's shop in Layerthorpe before school. After school it was straight home to help with the milking again. Mr. Bridge remembered that, in the winter it was always dark when he set off for school and often dark before he returned home at night. He recalled a Miss Bickle and a Miss Jenny Craig, teachers at the school. Miss Craig, he said, had married Mr. Foster, whose family had the provisions shop in East Parade for many years. He remembered also some of the farmers who lived down Malton Road when he was a young boy. There were the Spavin, Wrigglesworth, Butler and Woolons families. The latter family was part of Woolons and Harwoods, a business in Walmgate. This branch of the family bred bulldogs. He recalled Mr. Stephenson, auctioneer, at Barfield House and Mr. Popplewell at Rose Cottage, Malton Road. Mr. Popplewell was a dealer in cigars and also kept hackney ponies. In the 1930's he moved to the New Manor House down Stockton Lane. He remembered one farmer who was very rich but rather tight with his money. He and his family liked an evening at the theatre, but he would always make them walk there and back, in spite of having transport. Once, when it was very bad weather and pouring with rain, he refused their request to take a hackney cab home, although he could easily have afforded the fare. Unfortunately, his family took ill from this episode and he lost money then because he was without labour for a while. Another farmer, he recalled, employed a groom to look after his horses. His wife gave him some of his clothes because he was the same size. One day, however, he found that the groom had run off with all his clothes and also, his wife.[6]

Mrs. Dent's Memories

Mrs. Dent came to live in Heworth in a house in Second Avenue in the 1920's. She lived with her mother and father and baby brother, Billy. Her father had served in the 1st World War but suffered afterwards from the effects of gas poisoning. She attended Miss Hunter's school in Chestnut Avenue and remembered that the top of Chestnut Avenue and Dale's Lane was always full of puddles. Her best friends were David and Alec Kirk who lived down East Parade. Their father owned the big foundry in Peaseholme Green, later this became Adam's Hydraulics. She recalled going to see the big furnaces with the boys. She remembered also Granny Spink who lived next door to them, also the Triffet, Mansfield and Whincup families and Dr. Lythe at the Glen.

Her house in Second Avenue was a nice house she recalled. It had a nice drawing room and dining room with French windows that looked out down a long back garden. The bath was in the kitchen. It was a living kitchen with an old fashioned range to cook on. There was a sink in the scullery and a ducket toilet in a shed in the back garden. Her mother she remembered was very fond of reading novels, which she purchased from Bilborough's shop in Parliament Street. She had to spend a lot of her time looking after her brother Billy. When she could escape, she would wander across the fields, which stretched, from Main Avenue to the Tang Hall woods. She remembered catching tadpoles in the beck near Tang Hall Bridge and Mrs. Starkey from the Tang Hall chasing her and her friends. Her uncle, Henry Lund came round Heworth delivering bread. He carried the loaves on a trolley and children would beg rides on the handles.[7]

Mr. Bean's Memories

Mr. Noel Bean was born in 1916 at Sugar Hill Farm down Stockton Lane. His father was a market gardener. He remembers having to help feed the horses before school and when he returned home from school. He was always up at 6 a.m. and in bed before 10 p.m. He used to walk to Heworth School along Stockton Lane. He remembers Herbert's farmhouse and a small laundry in that area run by one of the Herbert family. This family would wash and starch collars and cuffs for a 1d and 2d he recalled. He remembers having to take a message to Yew Court, a big house opposite Whitby Avenue on Stockton Lane. It was occupied then by Mr. William Birch who had built this house of steel, because he was worried about fire. Later Mr. Billie Bridge lived there. He remembers Mr. Richardson, farmer and Mr. Fred Wilson of Heworth Village. Mr. Dixon was a joiner and undertaker and Mr. Pulleyn had a market garden off Hempland Lane. Whitby Avenue, he recalled, was a terrible road full of potholes. He remembers the carrier's cart that went to Stockton on Forest before there was a bus service. Mr. Thompson of Holtby Lane had the first motor service, an old Ford wagon. On a foggy night a man would walk in front of the wagon with an oil lamp. The Lee family who lived down Pasture Lane, then called Searchlight Lane, the Morrits of Ashfield Farm, and the Hagyards at Lady Cottage were just some of the neighbouring farmers.[8]

1st World War

Mr. Alan Audin remembers hearing about the bomb that dropped in Main Avenue in the 1st World War from his grandparents, Mr. and Mrs. Harding. When a zepplin raid was imminent, the gaslights were lowered and most people ran

Peace Party, Wood Street, 1919. These little houses were demolished in the 1970's and blocks of flats built. *(Courtesy of J. Murphy)*

into the surrounding fields. His grandparents used to run into Scobey's Fields he was told. Mr. Scobey had a farm near Heworth Vicarage. This farmhouse was demolished in the 1930's. On the night of the zeppelin raid in May 1916 on York, a stray bomb was dropped in Main Avenue, Heworth. The Hardings had run down the passage between the houses to the fields, but the impact of the bomb had dislodged the soot box that was kept there and covered the couple. When they arrived in the fields they were as black as "nigger minstrels" he was told.[9]

Mr. Bridge remembers the night the bomb dropped also. He recalled seeing the gable end of a house in Main Avenue damaged and the bed hanging out of the window. Fortunately no one was injured in Heworth that night but some people were killed in a lodging house in St. Saviour's Place by another bomb.[10]

Simpson's Nurseries

Before the houses were built in Forest Way, Stockton Lane, in 1937, this area consisted of nurseries owned by Mr. A Simpson. It specialised in cut flowers and decorative plants and ferns. As well as making wreaths and wedding bouquets, the nurseries furnished conservatories and drawing rooms. It provided flowers for all occasions such as balls, concerts weddings and private parties. Mr. Simpson employed deaf and dumb people to help work in the nurseries.[11] Mr. Simpson had married into the Empson family who had held land in Heworth since the early part of the 19th century.[12]

The Herbert Family

The Herbert family of Stockton Lane have been involved with milk delivery in the Heworth area since the early part of this century. They are related to the Herberts who were the licensees of the Nag's Head in Heworth Village. One branch of this family, Charlie Herbert, lived in a farmhouse on Stockton Lane, just past Lime Avenue, demolished 1970, to make a new housing development, Herbert's Way. Mr. Fred Herbert started delivering milk in the 1920's on a bicycle with a side box. He then acquired a bicycle from the Ebor Ice-cream Company, then a motor cycle and trailer and eventually a van.[13] The author remembers Mr. Herbert delivering milk to the bungalows on the Stray where she lived. Once, when she was late for school, he gave her a lift in his van. However she feared she may be even later for school as he had to deliver his milk bottles on the way, but he still managed to get her there on time.[14]

The Nag's Head Public House

Mr. and Mrs. William Herbert became mine hosts in late Victorian times, when the opening hours were 6 a.m. in the morning until 11p.m. at night. They held the licence for more than fifty years. Mrs. Herbert remembers when a shilling could buy five pints of beer, six drops of whisky or sixty cigarettes. When Mr. Herbert died in 1948, his widow, Mrs. Alice Herbert took over the running of the pub. She retired in 1952 aged 78 years and went to live in a cottage in Heworth Road nearby.[15]

The Hayes Family

Mr. John Robert Hayes, brother of the famous York photographer William Hayes, was born in 1876 in John Street, off Mill Lane. In the 1920's he had his grocery business at Mill House at the end of Harcourt Street, now a bank. This was probably the site of the old windmill. Miss Kathleen Hayes remembers as a child helping her father in the shop. Everything was kept in bulk then and all had to be weighed out. She remembers turning the handle of the big coffee-grinding machine. Her father delivered butter and eggs to Major Preston at Burnholme House. When the Major moved to Moreby Hall he delivered there as well.[16]

Mr. John Hayes outside his grocers shop at the junction of Harcourt Street and Hawthorn Grove. Circa 1920s. *(Courtesy of Miss K. Hayes)*

Chapter V. Notes and References.

1. Information. supplied by Mr. D. Poole, Penyghent Avenue.
2. Osbaldwick History Group. *Osbaldwick - A Suburban Village.* (1980) p.101.
3. Jenkinson, K. *York City Buses.* Autobus Review Ltd (1984) pp.10.11.
4. *Y. Gazette.* 1919. 1920. 1936.
5. Information supplied by Mrs. B, Poole, 6 Horsman Avenue.
6. Information supplied by Mr. N. Bridge, 20 First Avenue.
7. Information supplied by Mrs. Dent, 45 Grovesnor Terrace.
8. Information supplied by Mr. N. Bean, 1 Bean's Way.
9. Information supplied by Mr. A. Audin, Huntington, Mr. Bridge.
10. Y.R.L. *Y. Gazette.* 16. 5. 1916.
11. Y.R.L. *Kelly's Directories.* 1930.
12. N.R.R.O. *Register of Deeds.*
13. Information supplied by a Member of the Herbert Family.
14. Memories of Author.
15 *Y.E.P.* 11. Oct. 1952.
16. Information supplied by Miss K. Hayes, 30 Forest Way.

HEWORTH SCHOOL PUPILS
Mrs. N. Poole née Watson, front row, right. Circa 1910. *(Courtesy of Mrs. N. Poole)*

HEWORTH SCHOOL PT CLASS
Heworth School yard Circa 1930s. *(Courtesy of Mrs. E. Bradshaw)*

41

Mr. Ratcliffe (Headmaster) and pupils. Circa 1930s.   *(Courtesy of Mrs. E. Bradshaw.)*

Heworth School Choir. Circa 1930's.   *(Courtesy of Mrs. M. Bradshaw.)*

CHAPTER VI
Living in Heworth in the 1920's and 30's

What was it like to live in Heworth in the 1920's and 30's? A big difference in those times from today would be the presence of the overhead trolley lines for the trackless trolley buses. The trolley buses were introduced into Heworth after the 1st World War.

Heworth Village

The parade of houses just before the chapel began to be converted into shops during the 1930s. Mr. Bell had a small shop and Post office next to the chapel in the 1890's, but the rest were all private houses. This shop occupied the premises of a small cottage where Wesley House had once stood. It was demolished in 1977.[1]

Mrs. Sharpe remembers Walter Wilson's shop opening in the 1930's. She said all the children were given balloons and paper hats to advertise the new shop. Schoolboys would buy bags of dried peas from this shop to fill up their peashooters to fire at the girls.[2]

The Walnut Tree Villa was still a private house in the 1920's. Mr. John Richard Hill junior, a leather merchant, son of John Richard Hill senior, whose business was in James Street, still lived there and Mr. Frederick Wilson, a cattle dealer, lived at Hildreth House.[3] Colonel Cadill was at Chestnut House then called Tranent. Colonel Cadill died at this house in Heworth in 1930. He had entered the Royal Artillery in 1882 and served in various parts of the Empire and was promoted to Lieutenant-Colonel in 1900. He was in Salonika during the 1st World War. He was appointed Deputy Assistant Director of Remounts to the Northern Command at York after the war. He retired in 1927 and became a "Friend" of York Minster. His daughter, Miss Cadell, lived on at this house after his death.[4]

In the 1920's, some of the houses and cottages near the Walnut Tree were occupied by the Pulleyn, Varley, Haggard, Yorke, Speight and Sharman families. Mr. Dale lived at the White House in the 1920's and Mr. Knaggs lived there in the 1940's. At the end of Heworth Village, on Hempland Lane, was the Rectory belonging to St. Cuthberts. The house is still there but converted now into flats.[5] In the 1920's and early 30's, the Rev. Pyne lived there. He was very popular and a familiar figure riding his bicycle from the Rectory up Heworth Village to St. Cuthbert's Church. He always had a word for everyone and children loved to have a ride with him on his bicycle. After his death the Rectory was then moved to a house in East Parade.[6]

In the 1920's, there were only a few houses in Hempland Lane, Dixon's and Pulleyn's. Where Chapman's garage is today was Bland's yard and cottages.

Septimus Flower was the landlord in the early 1920's at the Britannia Inn. He was a coal merchant and haulage contractor and licensee of the Full Moon hotel in Walmgate before he came to Heworth. After his death his widow, Ada Flower, ran the Britannia. Their son founded Flower's Haulage business in Boroughbridge Road. The cottage adjoining the Inn, no 72, was used as a Cobblers Shop until the 1930's. In 1925 it was occupied by Mr. C. Poole, "Boot Repairer".

The Britannia Inn (closed 1964) showing the adjoining cottage and Trentholme. Circa 1910. *(Courtesy of J. Murphy)*

The Halliwell and later the Border families lived at the large house, Trentholme in the 1920's and 1930's which then had a very big garden. The semi-detached houses which ran up to the corner of Melrosegate, opposite the chapel, were not built until the 1930's. Previous to that tall trees fringed the edges of the garden that surrounded Heworth Cottage, demolished 1937.[7] Residents of Heworth Village remember the crows cawing in the tree tops. Heworth Hall was still there until 1934 although a new housing development, Heworth Hall Drive was started before the house was demolished and houses were built in the Hall's grounds.[8]

Monk Avenue Bungalows

Some of the detached bungalows that stand past the New Manor House, now called Monk Stray House, on land overlooking Monk Stray called Monk Avenue, were built in the 1920's. Mrs. Rankin's father, Mr. Harold Hearld, was one of the first to build his own bungalow in this area in 1922.

Mr. Hearld purchased a plot of land from the De Burgh estate agents and lived in a wooden 1st World War army hut in that area until he managed to have his own brick bungalow built. After the war army huts could be purchased quite cheaply and were often used to provide accommodation until better property was acquired or built. As well as those in Monk Avenue, there were a few wooden bungalows just past Hempland Lane corner before Whitby Avenue and some along Stockton Lane near Beans Way. The Linfoot family also lived a wooden bungalow overlooking Monk Stray until their brick bungalow was built. That wooden bungalow was adapted to make accommodation for two families. It remained in use until 1955, when it was demolished, providing space for two modern brick bungalows to be built.

Mrs. Rankin remembers the beck which ran along the rough track that was Monk Avenue, from the Manor House, past the bungalows to a pond at the end of Elmfield Terrace. The flats that are now next to the Manor House were not built until the 1970's. Mrs. Rankin recalled they had to use planks to cross the beck to reach their bungalow. The beck then ran from the pond across the Stray and disappeared under Malton Road. A small bridge was built across this beck in the middle of the Stray. The pond was always full of bullrushes and yellow flag iris flourished on the edges. The Stray she remembers was not drained and smooth as it is today but just rough grass and full of bumps and hillocks. It was used for pasturing cows and horses and the pasture master lived in the herdsman's cottage on Malton Road. In the spring the Stray was always full of buttercups, daisies and celandines.

There were smoother areas which were ideal for playing cricket and rounders. Mrs. Rankin recalled often being in trouble from her mother for rolling down the hillocks and getting cow dung in her hair. She said she thought the Stray was spoilt now it was drained and all flat and had lost a lot of wild character.[9]

The Pleausance

This was a private mental home, that stood in an area where Seymour Grove, a small cul de sac, near the top of Stockton Lane, stands today. It had previously been built as a private house, then, called Chestnut Grove, by the Cobb family. The grounds of this house extended up to the corner of Stockton Lane and Heworth Road. Dr. Leonard Baugh was the medical superintendent at the Home in the 1920's. He was the son of a plantation owner and was born at Kingston,

Jamaica. He came to England when he was seventeen and studied medicine and specialised in mental diseases. He was a medical Superintendent in Glasgow and Stirling and was in charge of five mental hospitals in France during the 1st World War. In addition to his practice in York, Dr. Baugh was a consultant alienist with chambers in Leeds. He was chairman of the York Rotary Club and President of Heworth Ward Conservative Association. After his death in 1933, the mental home closed and the grounds were used for building land.[10]

Mrs. Davies came to live at the first house built just past the old Police Station, in Heworth Road. Her husband built that house in the early 1930's. She remembers seeing the grounds and ruins of the Pleasaunce and the houses on Stockton Lane being built.[11]

Mrs. Rankin recalled the tall fencing that had surrounded the grounds of the mental home and the trees that fronted Heworth Road before the new houses were built. As a child she used to peep through holes in the fence to try and see the inmates. She also remembers the trees being cut down to widen Stockton Lane corner.[12]

Mrs. Sharpe's Memories

Mrs. Sharpe went to Heworth School in the 1930's. She recalled her time there. When she started at the school, the headmaster was a Mr. Ratcliffe and some of the teachers were Miss Morritt, Mr. Pratt and Miss Beverley, who was in charge of the infants. Mr. Rayson became the Headmaster after Mr. Ratcliffe. His speciality was singing and very young children had to sing his favourite songs, such as "Down among the Dead Men" and "Hearts of Oak". Not really suitable she thinks now for young children to sing. She remembers he did not like Bing Crosby or crooners in general. As the school was a church school it was very involved with the church. The Vicar at that time, a Canon Lamb, came over to give religious instruction. Each year, a summer garden party was held on the Vicarage lawn. The Vicarage was the big rambling house, now a Driving Test Centre, down Melrosegate, next to the church. The children from each class performed a dance to records on a wind up gramophone. The lawn was well cut and dry and the days also seemed to be warm and sunny, Mrs. Sharpe recalled. The children always had ice cream after the dances. Parents and friends sat around the lawn and were given cups of tea after the performance. Each year about Xmas time, the children performed dances and sketches in the school. The screens separating the classrooms were folded back to make a huge hall and a stage was put up. All the children were good at reading and writing and spelling "B"s were a regular feature of school days. She remembers beautiful coal fires in the school, and making pom-poms out of the cardboard tops of the milk bottles.

When George VI came to the throne, all the children in the school received a book, a mug and a tin of chocolates. She recalled the classroom in the Spring. Jam jars full of sticky buds and jars of frogspawn stood on the windowsills. From the open windows she heard the constant clip of horses hooves, hand bells and street cries, "coal", "milk" or "rabbit skins". Once a man with a horse pulling a roundabout came down the Village Street. The rides cost 1d and each child was given a sticky sweet, "A satin drop", after the ride. The owner stood on a platform in the middle of the roundabout and turned a big handle. On Friday afternoons, the teacher would read from a paperback book called "Enid Blyton's Sunny Stones". A nice ending to the school week, Mrs. Sharpe concluded.[13]

Mr. C. Poole's Memories

Mr. Chris Poole went to Heworth School in the 1930's also. The headmaster then was Mr. Ratcliffe, who was very proud of his school choir. Mr. Poole was a member of this choir, which won many competitions in York and the surrounding area. He remembers they often had impromptu rehearsals around the piano in spare moments between lessons.

Mr. Poole lived in Harrison Street when he was young and recalled playing in the fields near Dale's Lane. He remembers often seeing men suffering from shell shock around the village. There were always rag and bone men and pot men coming round the streets.[14]

Heworth Hall Drive

Mr. & Mrs. Goodwill came to live in a newly built house in Heworth Hall Drive in 1938. They had saved up hard to find the £30 deposit required for the house, which cost £600 and was built along with more houses by Mr. H. Williamson, builder. These houses were built in the old grounds of Heworth Cottage. Mr. Goodwill remembers the Cottage being demolished and the Barton family, the last occupants, going to live in East Parade. On the other side of Heworth Hall Drive there were houses already built. These had been erected in the grounds of Heworth Hall about 1928.

Mrs. Goodwill remembers that everything in her house was paid for in cash, no H.P. She recalled they had to wait for the house to be aired before moving in. Most of the houses on her side of Heworth Hall Drive were occupied by newly married couples and it was known as the "Brides side". She remembers Mr. Ellis from old Oakland Avenue delivering bags of coal to the houses. He always rang a bell she recalled. She remembers some of the people who lived in Heworth Village then. There were the Sharpe family who lived at Wesley House next to the Chapel, Colonel Smith at Yew Lodge and the Harrison, Pew, Richardson and Pulleyn families in the village houses.[15]

Burnholme Speedway

Burnholme House may have had a different future if the plans which were made for it in the 1930's had materialised. In 1930, the Burnholme Estate, comprising a fine country house, coach house and stables with 43 acres of land, had been purchased by a consortium of businessmen. They had great plans to lay a Speedway track, a quarter of a mile in length, with stands, on the eastern side of the Hall, where Burnholme Avenue is now. The existing coach house and stables would become an enclosure for competitors. The house itself would have facilities for tennis, badminton, squash, bowls and if there was enough interest, a small golf course was envisaged.

The Speedway track was laid with a safety fence and accommodation for 20,000 spectators. Mr. A. Temple was the local builder and Mr. F. Broadhead, who had formerly managed Wombwell Speedway, was the track manager. A social club was formed and opened on the 2nd of November 1930 when two hundred people attended a smoking concert. The club President was Mr. Reginald Hunt of the Aldwark Brewery and the chairman was Mr. C. Biscomb.

The first Speedway meeting was held on Good Friday, April 3rd 1931. Although the club had secured the services of well known riders such as George Reynard and Tommy Gamble, the project was set with misfortune. The weather that summer was very wet indeed, the annual rainfall for 1930 and 31 was in excess of 29" compared with an average 25". Attendances were lower than envisaged. One reason may have been the fact that the admission charges of 2/- and 1/- were double that charged by York City Football club. Also Burnholme was a little way out of York and most people did not have transport then. An announcement in the Yorkshire Evening Press of 6th August 1931 stated that the Speedway would have to close, due to a financial loss. " The Speedway is to close after next Monday. Negotiations are proceeding for the sale of the land. Bad weather delayed building of the track with the whole of last year spent on laying the concrete foundation. The first fixture was held on Good Friday in continual rain with the crowd below 2,000. Rain has threatened for most of the season. It is hoped an attempt is made to revive the sport". However, no one was prepared to take on the venture and within a short time the whole estate became a housing complex. Fortunately the Hall and the stables were saved. The Hall was converted into Burnholme Working Men's Club and the stables became a mews development.[16]

Burnholme Estate

After the Speedway closed, the land around Burnholme House was sold for building land. Mr. Joseph Norman Dunn was the owner architect for most of the houses that comprised, Burnholme Avenue and Drive, Langdale, Rydal, Woodside, Leyland and Gerard Avenues. Houses ranged from £600-£650 for special detached corner houses to £450 for a good semi-detached house in Leyland Road. There was also butcher's, greengrocer's, grocer's and newsagent's in Gerard Avenue.(17)

Miss Stanford remembers coming to live in Gerard Avenue in 1930 with her parents. She said that the housing in Bad Bargain Lane was mainly council, with only a few privately owned. There was a newsagent's shop, now the Post Office and a greengrocer's next door owned by John Hudson. The land beyond was mostly fields. She recalled the horses galloping in the fields opposite the first private houses in Bad Bargain Lane and Miss Cadell from Appletree Farm coming daily to collect cows for milking. The road then was just a mud track. Milk was delivered by Charlie Herbert twice a day, brought around in cans with a metal measure inside. Percy Gawthrop, who lived at 51 Bad Bargain Lane, was a local coal merchant As the building programme progressed, more shops appeared in Gerard Avenue with their own local character. Bill Barker became the local butcher and Frank and Elsie Fowler opened up their fish and chip shop (chips 1d and fish 2d). Frank Fowler was an ex-boxer and featured on cigarette cards of the time and Elsie his wife was an accomplished accordionist. Ray Drill had the newsagent's at first, without the Post Office and Mr. Hudson the greengrocer's. May Wilkinson and her father had a hairdressing business and William Cook a grocery business and bookies and Mr. Driver had a bakery, with home baked bread and cakes.

A Mr. Oliver came around with his handcart filled with fruit. He later progressed to a horse and cart. A fishmonger and baker she recalled were also regular traders in the area. Mr. Cox of the Shambles came around every Thursday collecting shoes for repair and in the summer, Ritchie's ice cream cart was a regular visitor.

As a child she remembers playing in the beck near the bridge and catching newts, tadpoles and sticklebacks. The hedges and fields on either side of Bad Bargain Lane were full of wild flowers and berries that she took to school for the nature table.

Gypsies often camped "up the lane" with their then traditional horse drawn caravans. The Gypsy women would come around the estate with their big baskets trying to sell their pegs and other wares.(18)

London's Newsagents

The big house, once called Millington House, now part of London's newsagency business, which still stands at the corner of Mill Lane and Hawthorn Grove, was built around 1870. In the 1890's, it was owned by the Millington family. After the death of Miss Joanna Ellen Millington the house and grounds were put up for auction in June 1920. It was described then as a valuable block of freehold property, comprising a detached house, then called Layerthorpe Grove, extensive grounds, three cottages, stables and outbuildings. This included the old mustard mill and cottage which stood on land at the side of Millington House fronting Mill Lane, then used as a laundry by Mr. Wright. Also another cottage, occupied then by a Mr. John Joy, with garden and large open yard was in the same area. The large gardens at the back of Millington House, which went nearly down to Layerthorpe Bridge, contained a stable and gardener's cottage called Hawthorn Cottage.[19]

Millington house was originally purchased by Mr. Arnold Rowntree, then bought from him by York Education Committee. Infants from St. Cuthbert's Road school in Layerthorpe were transferred there and it was used as a school until 1928 when the new Tang Hall schools were opened. Layerthorpe residents still remember going to that school, playing in the large gardens and seeing and smelling the apples stored in the upstairs' rooms. A part of the garden that contained the gardener's cottage was purchased at this time by Mr. Watson a builder. This cottage was demolished and the road that led to Layerthorpe Bridge was then called Hawthorn Grove. It had previously been known as Layerthorpe Road.[20] The big house, and most of the gardens, were bought by Mr. Albert London and his son Frederick in 1930. From this sale developed what is now known as London's Newsagents and Toyshop. Mr. London had originally opened his newsagency business in a shop in East Parade, now Threshers, in 1914. Mrs. Dent remembers buying comics and small toys in the 1920's at that shop. When they moved to the big house, Millington House, Mr. Albert London used to mend bicycles in the yard at the side of the house.[21] After the death of Frederick London, his widow, Mrs. Annie London and her sister in law Miss Beattie London ran the business together. Miss Beattie London was well known in music circles. She often played the organ at Heworth Chapel, was a member of York Symphony Orchestra and the Sayer Light Orchestra. She was also a keen gardener. The gardens behind London's shop were always a picture, with many flower beds and rose arbours. She was also one of York's examiners in life saving.

The business is run today by Frederick's son Derek, who in true family business tradition was born over the shop. As well as selling national and local papers and magazines, the shop today is also a thriving toyshop. It stocks a wide range of toys and garden play equipment as well as a good selection of greeting's cards, cigarettes and tobacco. Mr. London believes he offers as good a selection in his shop at competitive prices, as customers could get in the city centre. The one line that has remained constant over the years is the newspaper. Mr. London still employs many newsboys and girls, who deliver to hundreds of homes in the area.[22]

This was London's first shop on East Parade. It is now Thresher's Wine Shop.

(Courtesy of D. London)

EAST PARADE, HEWORTH, YORK.

Trolley Bus. Circa 1920.

(Courtesy of J Murphy)

East Parade and Mill Lane

Miss Jean Hempsall remembers the shops in East Parade in the 1930's. There was Wood's chemist, Olsen's fried fish shop and Mr. Shipp at Glen Stores, just past Glen Park. In Mill Lane, she recalled Mr. Wheatley, who had his garage where Crystal Garage is now, Hainsworth, Off Licence, and Mr. Simms at the Tea Time shop with the lovely bread cakes and potted meat She also remembers Mr. Foster, grocer and Mr. Oliver, greengrocer, and the fresh bread and cakes from Barton's cake shop in East Parade. She recalled also Mr. Tinson, builder, at the corner of Heworth Road and Mr. Danby with his taxis, which he kept in a yard at the back of South View. She also recalled the Harding family, they had a drapers business in High Ousegate, living at Montrose Villa, a large house next to South View and Mr. Day at the Post Office.

Mr. C. G. Wheatley took on the lease of a motor business in Mill Lane in the 1930's from a Mr. Robert Flower. In the early years this business was owned by Mr. J Taylor, a cab and carriage proprietor. Mr. Wheatley bought this business from Mr. Flower in 1944, but in the 1970's sold it to the Burmah Oil Company who then leased it to Crystal Motorist Discount centre.[23]

Mr. Frederick Wood opened his chemist shop in 1925 on East Parade then opened one in Heworth Village. At first the family lived above the shop. In 1966 they had six shops in York. Jack Wood was the only son. He was educated at Lime Tree School, Monk Bridge and then at Elmfield College. He was first elected Conservative councillor for Heworth Ward in 1952 and was Sheriff for York in 1961-2. He was very interested in Youth and Sports. He was President of York Rowing Club, York Light Opera Society and Heworth Cricket Club. He was also President of the Heworth Conservative Club, which had opened in East Parade in the 1920's as Heworth Constitutional Club.[24]

William Seale, owner of the now extinct brush and mat business in Low Petergate was a founder member of Heworth Conservative Club also. Although he had lived in Hungate as a boy, in the early years of this century he lived in East Parade. He died at his daughter's house in Heworth Hall Drive, at the grand old age of 99 years and 11 months, thwarted by 28 days on reaching his century.[25]

Mr. R. Newton opened his hairdresser's business in the front room of a house in East Parade in the late 1920s. During the war years his wife helped to run the business whilst Mr. Newton was in the Fire Service. At first it was just for ladies but after the war a small gent's shop was added. Betty Worrall was the first assistant. Today the Newton family is still very involved with the business and employs twelve or more staff including an osteopath, beautician and chiropodist.[26]

Heworth Green

Sir William Alexander Foster Todd lived at The Limes on Heworth Green in the early part of this century. He was a wine and spirit merchant and owned London's Hotel in Davygate. He was Lord Mayor four times in the 1st World War. He and his wife were familiar figures in the village. Mrs. Sharpe remembers that Mr. Foster Todd often wore a black coat with an astrakhan collar. Mr. Bridge recalled he once had to help bury his horse in the garden of The Limes near Heworth Road corner. Mrs. Foster Todd was also very fond of animals, and often gave parties for her dogs. Invitations were sent out to local dogs and the owners were asked to bring them at specific times. Dog races and treasure hunts were held in the grounds of The Limes. The owners were requested to pick them up at the end of the party and the dogs went home with party bags, "doggy bags".[27]

Eastern Villa became a school for girls in the 1930's. The principal was Miss Thompson. Clifton House became known as Heworth Hyrst and Dr. Reginald Dench, father of the celebrated actress, Dame Judi Dench, came to live with his family at No 54 Heworth Green, Dr. Dench opened up his medical practice there originally with Dr. Kelly and Dr. Burrows. Heworth residents remembers seeing the Dench family returning from their cycle rides in the country.

Heworth Moor House became a nursing home in the 1930's. The first matron was Miss Jessie Thorne. Later it became a home for unmarried mothers run by the Diocesan Association of Moral Welfare. Mr. Perry had the little newsagent's shop "The Kiosk" in part of the old bus shelter at the top of Stockton Lane.[28]

Heworth Grange Estate

After Mr. Moiser of Heworth Grange died, much of the land that had formed part of this estate, which stretched over what is now Dodsworth Avenue and Pottery Lane area, was sold to York Corporation. A council estate was started in the 30's and re- housed a number of Layerthorpe residents. Many of the houses in the small yards and terraces in Layerthorpe, like John Bull Yard and Layerthorpe Buildings that led to the Foss were demolished at this time.[29] The large detached houses that run along Heworth Green, just past Dodsworth Avenue to Malton Road corner, were built at this time also. Heworth Croft became a hostel for St. John's College in the 1930's. Dalguise House, turned into flats in the 1920's, was demolished in the 1930's and a new housing development, Dalguise Grove, was built in the grounds.[30]

Burnholme Working Men's Club

In the early 1930's, several local men, Cyril Robinson, Jack Sturdy, Bill Flowers and Doug Stanford, approached club breweries with a view to buying Burnholme House and making it into a Working Men's Club and social club. This was approved and the Club was officially opened on November 21 1935. The ceremony was performed by Mr. J. W. Wilson, President of the York and District Club's Brewery. The Club was decorated with the colours of York's two senior football teams, chocolate and cream (City's old colours) and amber and black, Rugby league colours. The first President was Arthur Willis followed by H. Kitchen, A. Craven, and T. Sumpton. Other club committee members in these early times were Jack Sturdy, Doug Stanford and W. Flower. There was also a cricket, angling and bowls section. Miss Stanford remembers the tables and umbrellas out on the lawns in the summer. There were also many trips and parties for member's children. She remembers the Christmas parties with a ventriloquist, Billy Bell. There was also a thriving tennis club.[31]

Mr. Newton outside his hairdresser's shop in East Parade. Circa 1930s.

(Courtesy of the Newton Family)

Chapter VI. Notes and References.

1. *Y.E.P.* 1920-1930.
2. Information supplied by Mrs. A. Sharpe, 27 Heworth Road.
3. Y.R.L. Murray, H. *Pedigrees of York Families.*
4. *Y. Gazette.* 1933.
5. *Kelly's.* 1920-1930.
6. Webster. A. E. *Looking Back at Layerthorpe* (1996). Q.E.D. p.49.
7. *Kelly's.* 1920-1930.
8. Information supplied by Mrs. Sharpe.
9. Memories of Mrs. E. Rankin, 15 Monk Avenue.
10. *Y. Gazette.* 1933.
11. Information supplied by Mrs. Davies, 39 Heworth Road.
12. Memories of Mrs. E. Rankin, 15 Monk Avenue.
13. Memories of Mrs. Sharpe.
14. Information supplied by Mr. C. Poole, 115 Stockton Lane.
15. Information supplied by Mr. and Mrs. Goodwill, 5 Heworth Hall Drive.
16. Poole, D. *Speedway in York.* Y.A.Y.A. Times(1990). *Y.E.P.* 1930-37.
17. Information supplied by Mr. W. Maddison, Mill Lane.
18. Memories of Miss L. Y. Stanford, 50 Bad Bargain Lane.
19. *Y.E.P.* 3.6.1920.
20. Webster. A. E. op. cit. 6.
21. Memories of Mrs. Dent, 45 Grosvener Terrace.
22. *Y.E.P.* 30.5.75. Additional information supplied by Mr. D. London, Chestnut Avenue.
23. Information supplied by Miss J. Hempsall, 48 Hewley Avenue. Information supplied by Mr. P. Wheatley.
24. Y.R.L. Murray, H. *Pedigrees of York Families.*
25. Information supplied by Mr. D. Poole, 19 Penyghent Avenue.
26. Information supplied by Mr. C. Newton, East Parade.
27. Information supplied by Mrs. M. Poole, 115 Stockton Lane.
28. *Kelly's.* 1930. Memories of Author.
29. Webster. A E. op cit. 6.
30. Y.C.A. *York C.Council Minutes.* 1920-30.
31. Memories. Miss Y. Stanford. *Y. Gazette and Herald* 2.8.1952.

CHAPTER VII
TO CHURCH OR CHAPEL

Early Methodists

Methodism was brought to Heworth by John Nelson a Birstal stonemason. He had been press-ganged into the army and it was whilst he was quartered in York that he preached on Heworth Moor on May 13th 1744. John Wesley came to York in 1747 and after that date, Methodism grew in the city. A chapel was erected in Peaseholme Green in 1759, and one in New Street in 1805.[1] In that same year class no 14 was formed in Heworth led by W. Robinson of Stockton on Forest, with members T. and C. Wilkinson, Martha O'Neil, T. Botterill, and Paul Batty of Heworth.

The First Chapel

A small chapel was built in Heworth Village in 1826. It stood further back from the road than the present chapel and had a rather barn like exterior. In the 1820's a Mr. Boggitt had built a house to the east of the chapel called Heworth House. He was a shoe maker and was very involved with the chapel in these early years. This family was related to the Boggitts of Huntington. Mr. Cooper, Mr. Groves, Mr. Thackeray and Mr. Stoker were the mainstay of the chapel in these early times.[2]

The New Chapel

In the 1860's, William Leak, a prosperous draper, came to live at the Glen in East Parade. He was a very staunch Methodist. He often complained that the old chapel was small and damp and wanted to help build a new one. His widow, Mrs. Hannah Compton Leak left a bequest in her will to enable Heworth Methodists to do just that. Designed by Edward Taylor, the new chapel was in a perpendicular gothic style, fashionable at this time. The property that stood to the east of the old chapel, Mr. Boggitt's old house, Heworth House, then occupied by Mr. Bell, was demolished. The new chapel stood partly on this site and partly on the site of the old chapel. The transept of the old chapel served as a schoolroom and could be cut off from the main chapel by sliding doors. During the time the old chapel was demolished and the new chapel built, services were held in the sitting room of the Glen. The foundation stone of the new chapel was laid on December 11th 1889 by John F. Taylor, one of the great worthies of Victorian Methodism in York. William Camidge started the first Sunday School in the new building, assisted by Mr. Hayward and Mr. Bell and later on Mr. Hagyard.[3] The families of Mr. John Richard Hill, a leather merchant, and John Booth were very involved with the chapel. Mr. Hill had come to live at the Walnut Tree Villa in late Victorian times. He married Hannah, eldest daughter of John Booth of Beech House Heworth. (This is the cottage just before the Walnut Tree). John Booth started as an apprentice at Leak and Thorp, eventually becoming a partner in the firm.[4] Mr. Robert Kay, organist and choir master, took over the running of the Sunday School helped by Mr. Pulleyn, the owner of the nurseries which were behind the chapel. Mrs. Twinam started a junior class about this time also.[5]

The Glen.   (*Courtesy of City of York Library*)

Sunday School Memories

In the 1930's, it was decided to pull down the back premises of Wesley House and to build a schoolroom in the yard to cater for extra children. A Junior Guild was started in 1937 with Mr. W. E. Smith as warden. It was at this time also that the Hayes Family was very involved in the life of the chapel.

Mrs. J. Southwood remembers being a Sunday School teacher in the 1930's. She also joined the Junior Guild. Her mother, Mrs. Coatesworth, was one of the founder members of a woman's meeting (the Bright Hour).[6] The author remembers going to Sunday School in the early 1940's. Her teachers were Miss Kathleen Hayes, Miss J. Hempsall and Miss Janet Raines. The Superintendent of the Sunday School was Mr. W. Smith. She remembers Mrs. Evelyn Hayes playing the organ and the boy who pumped the old organ, he was always hidden behind the curtain. She recalled old Mr. Hayes attending services. After his death, the family presented the present altar table in his memory. The highlight of the chapel year was to her, the Sunday School anniversary. A big platform was erected over the altar area and all the children would sit in their best clothes waiting their turn to sing or recite. Every one had special programmes and the chapel was full of flowers. All the parents were invited and the services took place all weekend and Monday evening.[7]

Mr. D. Reeder remembers going to the Sunday School in the 1940's also. He recalled the chapel with the old boxed pews and side aisles. He remembers signing the pledge, attending lantern talks with lantern slides on foreign countries, Christmas parties and outings. The high spot for him was giving recitations in the main chapel, in special services. He joined the Junior Guild and remembers social evenings and the occasional gatherings in the evening without adult supervision. This occasionally led to high jinx's, a battle with an old set of hymn books and playing Postman's knock in the vestry.[8]

Later Years

In the 1960's, Mr. G. E. Jackson joined Heworth, after the closure of the Duke of York Mission Rooms in Layerthorpe. He was a very enthusiastic junior choir master and helped to start a youth club in 1964. The Bowman, Hill, Hutchinson, Russell, Riley, Porter and Wrightson families were just some of the families that were very involved in the chapel in these years. Mr. Harold Haw was the leader of the adult choir, 1952 to 1981.

During these years it was decided to pull down Wesley Cottage, where the caretakers, the Sharpe family, had lived and rebuilt new Sunday School premises. The new building was ready by 1967 and the opening ceremony was performed by Helen Wrightson and Glen Wright, presided over by Mr. Andrew Hutchinson the new Superintendent. Mr. Smith had resigned after giving forty years service.[9]

The Chapel Today

Today, the chapel has many activities including a Toddler group, Young Wives and Mums and Baby group. The Wesley Guild is still active, Mr. Paddy Gibson has been the Secretary since 1956. Mr. Eric Wrightson, Miss K. Hayes and Miss J. Hempsall are still very involved with the life of the chapel and there are many other families who have been supportive members of the chapel for a long time. In 1990, the chapel was altered again, to provide a place for meetings and services. The chapel today provides a centre where prayers can be said and help given to anyone that is sick or in need.[10]

Heworth Church

No church had existed in Heworth, of which we have knowledge, before 1869. The inhabitants had to attend three separate city churches, All Saints,

Peaseholme, St. Olaves, or St. Saviour's. In 1586, All Saints was united with St. Cuthberts. The Rectory for this parish was situated at the bottom of Heworth Village. The first Sunday School for the church was held in the stable block of Heworth Cottage. Between 1867-1869 a church was finally built in Heworth. The Rev. Joscelyn Willey and later his widow were greatly instrumental in building this church. It was built of stone in the early English style and comprised of a nave and chancel with a tower in the north east angle of the nave. The architect was G. Fowler Jones and it cost £6,436 and had accommodation for 280 adults and 134 children. There was also a large wooden reredos made in Oberammergau.

The Gifts

Lady Wheler contributed £5,000 and Mrs. Starkey of the Tang Hall gave an alms dish. The stained glass centre window, showing the Ascension of Christ, was a gift from Mrs. Bell in memory of her husband. The builder, Mr. Keswick, gave the stained glass centre window at the east end of the church. The foundation stone was laid by Sir Trevor Wheler in 1867 and he gave to the church the massive oak communion table, but had alas died before the Consecration in 1869.[11]

Early Days

In the early years of this century the vicar was the Rev. Albert Victor Jones. He was the vicar from 1908-1930. There were many church activities at this time. There were bible classes for men and women, mothers meetings, Band of Hope and Sunday School. Many were held in the Church Institute, a wooden building situated near Main Avenue. Some of the families who were the mainstay of the church at this time were the Coton, Foster, Gray, Griffiths, Hagyard, Laycock-Brown, Rawlings, Shackleton and Wheatley families. Mr. J. Howard Gray was the organist for many years and Miss Dalton did stirling work with the running of the Sunday School classes, assisted by Miss Butterfield.[12]

The New Church Hall

The new Church Hall was built by T. and M. Caffrey, Heworth builders, in 1935. It stood in Melrosegate, opposite the Vicarage, in what had been part of Heworth Hall grounds. The foundation stone was laid by the Lord Mayor of York and dedicated by the Bishop of Whitby on the 12 October 1935. Special services were held over that weekend and a Grand Bazaar held during the following week. The new Church Hall was home to the Mother's Union, Girl Guides, Church Lad's Brigade, Sunday School. and Scripture Union.[13] The latter was run by Sydney Oglesby who claimed to have known 1,000 children by name. Mrs. Foster remembers going to Scripture Union in the 1940's. She recalled they had to take pennies to help buy bricks to build a new church, St. Wulstan's in Fossway.[14]

Church Lad's Brigade

Mr. C. Poole was a member of the Church Lad's Brigade in the 1940's. They had a big drum and bugle band and each Sunday they marched round the parish. They held gymnastics in the Church Hall and an annual camp at Fadmoor he recalled. The initiation ceremony among the lads was that of having to be bumped down the cellar steps and thrown into a holly bush. He remembers singing in the church choir in the 1930's when the church was all lit up with gas flared lights.[15]

Heworth Scouts

The First Heworth Scout group was formed on December 1st 1919. The group first met in a room above Victorian stables attached to the Vicarage. Access was by a ladder. In 1931, the scouts moved to a room above lock up garages between the school and the police station in Heworth Road. The group consisted of a Scout troop, Wolf Cub pack and Rover crew. The uniform was navy shirt and shorts and stockings with maroon scarves and white lanyards.
In the 1940's, the Group Scoutmaster was Mr. A. E. Smith better known as "Fox". He was the second Scoutmaster, the first was Mr. I. Spence. Mr. Smith started his scouting in 1919 when he was then a Troop leader.

In 1933, a party from Heworth met their founder Baden Powell. In 1934, representatives attended the first National St. George's Day service in St. George's chapel and took part in the march past before King George V and Queen Mary. In the 1940's, Mr. Smith was ably assisted by assistant Scoutmasters, A. E. Watson (Brock), J. P. Ryan (Panther) and Troop Leader, J. Moffat. The troop had three patrols then, the Owls under Patrol Leader Sydney Paxman, Woodpeckers, K. Warwick and Badgers Patrol Leader, R. Keighley. The Wolf Cub pack was run by Cub master Miss M. L. Smith who was the Akela for many years.

The scouts had an annual camp at Brockfield Hall. They were reliant on subscriptions and help from the Parent's committee for the purchase of equipment. In the 1950's, a large wooden hut was bought for the scouts by a unknown benefactor and placed on a site situated in Littte Bad Bargain Lane. Later, with lots of help and support from numerous parents and fund raising activities, the group managed to have built a more permanent brick Scout Hut.[16]

Guides and Brownies

Mrs. Bainton was in charge of the Guides in the 1940's. The weekly meetings were held in the Church Hall. Mrs. S. Sykes remembers attending Guide meetings and working for Guide badges. She recalled going out on trekking expeditions and learning to light fires, without matches, near Tang Hall Beck.

The author was a Brownie in the 1940's also. She recalled learning to tie knots and playing games in the church hall. Once at Xmas time, the Brownie pack went carol singing around the village and took little presents to several old people. However, although it was only early evening some people had gone to bed. In those days when there was no television, people often retired early, to save fuel and electricity.[17]

Heworth Scouts at Brockfield Park. Circa 1940s.   *(Courtesy of Mr. S. Paxman)*

Second Heworth Guide Company. Church Parade, Sunday morning 1960 Captain Mrs. H. Robinson.

Chapter VII. Notes and References.

1. P. M. Tillot (ed). Victoria County History. *The City of York* (1961) p.412
2. Camidge, W. *Methodism in York,* Weslyan Methodist Conference. York. 1908.
3. Royle, E. *Methodism in Heworth.* Quacks (1990).
4. Y.R.L. *York Cuttings Book* (1900-1910)
5. Information supplied by Mrs. Beaumont (née Kay), Lamel Beeches York.
6. Information supplied by Mrs. J. Southwood, 11 Hempland Lane.
7. Information supplied by Mrs. Appleton (née Reeder).
8. Information supplied by Mr. D. A. Reeder, 17 Chantry Hurst, Epsom.
9. Memories of Mrs. O'Neill (née Webster), Isle of Man.
10. Information supplied by Mrs. Bowman, Hempland Avenue.
11. Tillot (ed). op cit 1 p.403
12. Y.R.L. Y/283. *Heworth Church Newsletter.* (1940)
13. Y.R.L. Y/283. *Heworth Parish Church Brochure.* (1935)
14. Y.E.P. 11.10.1952. Memories of Mrs. J. Foster (née Carney).
15. Information supplied by Mr. C. Poole, Stockton Lane.
16. Information. Mr. S. Paxman (late), Huntington Road.
17. Memories of Mrs. S. Sykes (née Carney) and Mrs. A. Appleton.

CHAPTER VIII
LIFE IN WARTIME HEWORTH

War is declared

World War II was declared on Sunday the 3rd September 1939. Many people in York heard Mr. Chamberlain make his famous announcement on the wireless, others heard it in the churches. The author's mother, Mrs. E. Reeder remembers standing outside York Minster when it was announced that England was now at war with Germany. Many people started crying and hugging one another she recalled.[1] Plans for Conscription and a National Register of Occupations had been drawn up by the Government, prior to the outbreak of War. Blackouts, sirens and other wartime precautions were begun. Windows had to be covered with suitable blackout materials or stuck up with brown paper. There was no school on the next Monday morning as many teachers had been called up. Parents were told to look in the local newspapers for notices to say when schools would re-open. Many schools were closed for reorganisation. Everyone was issued with gas masks and instructed to take them everywhere they went at all times. Young children had Mickey Mouse masks and special masks were provided for babies. Under the terms of the Emergency Power's (Defence) Act 1939, amended in 1940, the Government took control of people's daily life and labour. A full and efficient work force was organized and many women found themselves working for the first time, having to take jobs in Industry, Agriculture and the Armed Forces. Many women remember working at Rowntree's factory making munitions. Although most men between the ages of 18-40 were called up, there were some in Reserved Occupations such as the Railway that were exempt.[2]

Evacuees

Evacuation began before the war started, but it was announced in the newspapers that this was a precautionary measure, not that war was inevitable. Schoolchildren, pre-schoolchildren with mothers and priority cases like expectant mothers were evacuated from towns that were thought to be at risk from bombings, such as Manchester, Sheffield, Leeds, Hull and Newcastle to the York area. York City itself was on the reserve list, so most evacuees went to the suburbs and nearest villages. Heworth Without received evacuees, who, after arriving at Haxby, were brought to a meeting place near Galtres Avenue, Stockton Lane.

The author remembers coming to York from Hull as an evacuee on 1st September 1939. No one knew where they were going and the train was constantly being diverted from the main line. After a long journey, she remembers her mother was surprised to find that they were only at Haxby, York. She thought they must be at least in Scotland. The author, mother and brother were billeted at Clifton for a while but the author's mother could not get on with the lady of the house. She remembers being instructed by her mother to look in the dustbin to see what the host family had had to eat for tea as her mother complained that they were only fed "Bully Beef " known better as corned beef. After many changes of billets they eventually returned home to Hull.[3] By January 1940, 61% of all evacuees had returned home for various reasons. The main reason being that nothing really happened at first, no bombing raids occurred and it was dubbed the "Phoney war".

Mr. Pearson. A.R.P. warden, showing Heworth residents how to extinguish incendiary bombs. *(Courtesy of Mrs. S. Elmer)*

Rationing and Ration Books

Petrol rationing was introduced in 1939, food rationing began in Jan 1940 and clothes in 1941. Everyone was issued with a ration book and had to register at a provisions shop. By 1942 the rations for one adult for one week would be: One shilling and twopence worth of meat, approx. 1lb 8oz Cheese, 4oz Bacon, 8oz Fats, 8oz Sugar, 4oz Jam or Marmalade, 2 - 4 Eggs and 4 - 6 pts of Milk. The Ministry of Food published new ways to prepare meals and introduced new sources of protein. The author remembers her mother bringing home whale meat, horse meat and snook instead of salmon. None of these were very palatable. There were many recipes using dried eggs and dried milk. Everyone was encouraged to grow their own vegetables and "Dig for Victory" was a popular slogan. Chickens and rabbits were kept in backyards and gardens and pigs kept on allotments.[4] The author remembers her mother preserving eggs in waterglass and bottling pounds of tomatoes, onions and red cabbage to help out the weekly rations.[5]

A.R.P.'s and Air Raid Shelters

After Dunkirk, the Local Defence Volunteers were formed. This was a voluntary service for men aged 17/65yrs who where not on active service. At first it was rather amateurish and known locally as the " Look, Duck and Vanish Brigade". Later the " Home Guard " as it eventually became known was more organized and professional and played an important role in the defence of the nation. Many women as well as men gave up their spare time to become A.R.P. wardens or firewatchers. Warden posts and centres where set up all over the city. In the Heworth area there was a warden's post in Dale's Lane, Hempland Lane, the junction of Heworth Green and Dodsworth Avenue and an A.R.P. Depot in Foss Island's Road.[6]

Mr. Newbold remembers the A.R.P. post on waste land in Dale's Lane. It was manned during the day by regulars and in the evening by volunteers who would collect the key from his house in Clarke's Terrace. He recalled a Mr. Sykes, Mr. Gravil and a Miss Wilson who were regulars and Mr. Baram and Mr. Griffiths, volunteers. If the "purple light" appeared then they would all go home. However no sooner had they all gone home, the siren would sound and they would all have to return. He also remembers people fire watching at the back of Mr. Huitson's Off Licence in Heworth Road. This was handy for drinks to keep out the cold and keep spirits up.[7]

Mrs. Southwood remembers working at a fire sub station set up in a hut in the yard behind South View down East Parade. She was actually employed at the Railway offices but had to do some work for the war. She worked two evenings a week. She recalled also men fire watching on top of the gasometer in Layerthorpe. They would ring up the fire station to tell them when they had arrived safely at the top.[8]

Miss Sheila Elmer remembers her dad , Mr. Bill Pearson, being a full time group centre A.R.P warden in Heworth. The centre was a converted house in the row of shops in East Parade opposite Newton's hairdressing shop. Among other duties, he received the "Red Alert" when enemy planes were imminent and had to engage the switch which activated the siren placed on the gasometer near Foss Bridge, likewise the "All Clear".[9]

Burnholme Club was also used as an A.R.P. centre. Firewatchers took up residence in a little cellar next to the boiler room. At the beginning of the war the building had been taken over by the army for billets. This did not interrupt the normal life of the club and the lads were made Honorary Members.[10]

Although York was considered relatively safe from the threat of the Luftwaffe, it still had to prepare itself for air raids. Some people had Morrison shelters, rather like steel cages, which could contain a bed, erected in their houses. Others had Anderson shelters built in their gardens. Mrs. Foster remembers a Morrison shelter erected in the passage between the houses in Tang Hall Lane. Mrs. P. Davies recalled the one in her garden down Heworth Road. It was entered by steps and contained everything you needed to stay in for a while, beds, stove and food supplies.[11] Mr. Newbald remembers that his neighbours, Mr. and Mrs. Wilkinson had one at the bottom of their garden in Harrison Street. Large brick shelters were placed at the end of most main roads. The author remembers one that stood near her house on the Stray, Monk Avenue. Some people in Heworth remember the shelters on wasteland at the corner of Melrosegate and Heworth Village, opposite the Chapel and the ones at the back of Glen Park. Rowntrees provided shelters for their workers underneath their dining block and schools often had shelters in the school yards. Mr. Newbald recalled the one in Heworth School yard.[12]

Air Raids

Although York was not bombed as much as neighbouring cities such as Sheffield, Leeds and Hull, sirens sounded in the city 138 times. There were eleven air strikes in which high explosives and incendiary bombs were dropped. In August 1940, two ladies were seriously injured by a bomb that dropped in the Osbaldwick Lane area, one lady subsequently died. In October of the same year four bombs were dropped in the Elmfield Avenue, Malton Road area. Two bombs fell in a farmyard of Thorn Nook and damaged a cow byre. The third bomb fell in the front garden of 11 Sefton Avenue. Two men, John March of 9 Sefton Avenue and Henry Coles, 22 Sefton Avenue, both part time wardens, were killed instantly. In January 1941, an enemy aircraft passed over the city and dropped incendiary bombs in a line extending from Hull Road to Peaseholme Green, causing fires and damage to property. On this occasion, bombs were dropped in the Heworth area, causing damage to a house in East Parade. A bomb also dropped near the Gas works near Monk Bridge but there were no casualties from this raid.[13]

The Baedeker Raid

Fortunately Heworth escaped most of the bombs that fell on York in the Baedeker Raid on the 29th April 1942. This raid was a reprisal mission after

British forces, under the newly appointed Air Marshall Sir Arthur "Bomber" Harris had ordered raids on the medieval towns of Luebeck and Rostock in Germany. Goering's Chief of Staff used the Baedeker Guide to Britain to select targets of equal historical and cultural importance. York was very lightly defended but had the railway, at this time a vital link with Hull docks, which carried supplies to Russian allies overseas. Many Heworth residents remembers this raid. They saw the flares coming down on the city and saw the enemy bombers, heard the screeching of the bombs and witnessed the fires that lit up the sky. As well as the station area, Bootham, Clifton, Burton Stone Lane and Poppleton Road took the brunt of the bombing that night. Seventy-nine people where killed, eighty four seriously injured and one hundred and twenty slightly injured and there was a lot of damage to houses and buildings.[14] A bomb dropped in Mansfield Street, Layerthorpe, destroying three houses and killing one person. The John Bull Public House, was damaged, nearby houses and Bilton Street School were damaged also that night. Mr. Newbald remembers a boy in his class, Roy Batters, from Mansfield Street, being bombed out then. The people, who had been bombed out in that area were brought to Heworth School, so the school children had a holiday the next day.[15] Mr. A Reeder from Heworth, an engine driver, arrived at the Railway Station minutes after this attack to start his shift. He helped to put out the fires in the station yard. He propped up his bicycle before he began work, but when he returned for it he realised he had placed it against an unexploded bomb.[16]

Leisure and Lights Out

The government encouraged a wide range of entertainments during the war years to take people's minds off the bombings and to keep up morale. After an initial closure at the start of the war, the cinemas and theatres reopened and were filled to capacity. The cinemas were opened for the first time on Sundays to cater for the large number of service men stationed in and around York. There were ten cinemas in York at this time and most changed the films midweek. There were regular dances, concerts and many social functions. The De Grey Rooms, Albany Ballroom and dances in Rowntree's dining block, were popular venues.

Many married women, especially those whose husbands were away, as well as unmarried women, frequented the dance halls to dance with the Free French, Canadian and American airmen. The author remembers that her mother and Aunt, who was living with them whilst her husband was away, loved to go dancing at the Albany Ballroom. They met many service men and she recalled a Frenchman calling round home in an old battered car, hoping to take her Aunt out for a spin. However, the author's father insisted that all the children had to accompany them. Many a time they all ended up having to push the car when it ran out of petrol. Rabbit pie suppers and "Knees Up" were popular activities in the war years. The author remembers going regularly to a house in Bad Bargain Lane, to her mother's friend, for lovely rabbit pie suppers. She recalled playing George Formby records and one record called "In a Monastery Garden" on an old wind-up gramophone. Her mother was always called up to recite and "The Green Eye of the Idol of Katmandu" and exerts from "The Rubaiyat of Omar Khayyam" were her particular favourites. The evening generally ended with a sing song around the piano and dancing to "Knees up Mother Brown" and the" Hokey Cokey".[17]

All children were involved with the war effort. Picking rose hips for Rose Hip syrup and collecting waste paper for salvage, were popular activities for children. Everyone was encouraged to save for "York Warship Week "and "Wings Week". For every 2/6p saved per week, one hundred savings bonds were contributed to the war effort. Mr. Newbald remembers making posters at school for "York Wings Week". He also recalled a German aircraft on display in Parliament Street and a barage balloon on Heworth Golf course.[18]

V.E. Celebrations

Peace in Europe was declared on 5th May 1945 and there were great plans to celebrate V. E. Day. Most streets had their "street party" and fancy dress parades. Mrs. Sykes remembers a V.E. party she and her sister attended at the Tang Hall hotel. Mrs. Murray remembers one held at the Walnut Tree. There were games, races and fancy dress competitions.[19] The author recalled going to pick up the 'chicken bits' from her mother's friend's house that day. She passed many streets in Heworth having their parties, the tables set out, loaded with jellies, cakes and ice cream, rare treats. Her mother had refused her request to have a street party where she lived, saying there were too few houses and it wasn't a "street", but she now believes it was because her mother and Aunt wanted to go into town and share in the celebrations there. Many people remembered the dancing in Parliament Street that went on all night.

Mr. Newbold remembers the V.E. party that was held in Harrison Street. There was fancy dress and a trellis table loaded with jellies and ice-cream and home-made cakes. Every one made a special effort, even though everything was still rationed. In the evening he went to stay with his aunt, who had a flat in Parliament Street and he remembers seeing the dancing in the streets from the bedroom window.[20]

(Courtesy of Mr. R. Newbold)

V.E. Celebrations, Harrison Street.

V.E.Party Harrison Street. 1945.

Chapter VIII. Notes and References.

1. Memories of Mrs. E. Reeder (late Speculation Street).
2. *Y.E.P.* 25.9.1939.
3. Information supplied by Author and the late Mrs. Reeder.
4. *Y.E.P.* 1939-1945.
5. Memories of Author.
6. Y.R.L. North Yorkshire. C.C. *Document Pack World War 2.*
7. Memories of Mr. Newbald, 91a Heworth Village.
8. Information supplied by Mrs. J. Southwood, 11 Hempland Lane.
9. Information supplied by Mrs. S. Elmer, 1 Martin Cheeseman Court.
10. *Y. Gazette and Herald.* 2.8.1952.
11. Information. Mrs. J. Foster and Mrs. Davies, 39 Heworth Road.
12. Memories Author and Mr. Newbald.
13. Op Cit. 6.
14 York Oral History Group. *Through The Storm.*
15. Memories of Author and Mr. Newbold.
16. Memories of Mr. A. T. Reeder (late Monk Avenue)
17. Memories of Mrs. Greear (late Hempland Lane), Mrs. Appleton.
18. Information supplied by Mr. Newbold.
19. Memories of Mrs. Sykes Mrs. Murray, Heworth Village.
20. Information supplied by Author and Mr. Newbold.

CHAPTER IX
GROWING UP IN THE 40'S

Food Shortages

The years after the end of the 2nd World War were full of problems for the new labour government elected in 1945. The country was very much in debt and there were great fuel and food shortages. Rationing became even tighter and people still had to queue for food. In 1945, everyone was allowed 1lb of oranges per week and a mark stamped on the ration books. Shopkeepers in York complained that some people had tried to rub out the marks to obtain more oranges. However, most people were content with their lot and just happy to have the war over.[1]

Bad Weather

The years immediately after the war, 1945, 1946 and 1947 had very bad winters. In 1945, there were 23 degrees of frost recorded in January and there was skating on the lake in Rowntree's Park and the River Ouse froze over. In 1947, there were heavy snow falls and strong gales. In February of that year buses were stranded on Garrowby Hill and a food train was sent out from Driffield to Malton. Men on horse back met the train at Malton and delivered food parcels to villages on the Wolds, like Wetwang, Fimber, Wharam and Burdale. Conditions were so bad that the Mountain Rescue teams had to be called out to help villages cut off by snow.[2]

York Floods 1947

Because there had been so much snow in the hills around York, when the thaw came in March, excess water was brought down to the River Ouse at York. Most of the areas adjacent to the river, such as Clifton and Leeman Road , were badly flooded straight away. The water in the River Foss and the becks that led off it, such as Tang Hall beck, also flooded the surrounding area. Tang Hall was virtually cut off, and Burnholme Estate was also in flood that year. The inhabitants of the houses down Tang Hall Lane, near Tang Hall Bridge, were virtually marooned.[3]

A report in the *Yorkshire Evening Press* stated that the Lang, Emmell and Agar families were the worst affected on account of the Tang Hall beck rising 20ft. A wooden jetty was erected on the junction of Tang Hall Lane and Wolfe Avenue. A ferry boat service, operated by Corporation employees, took food to the houses. Milk was delivered daily, but often lost in the floodwaters. The marooned families stated that, they were all well, were able to make a cup of tea and passed the time playing cards. The local fuel office commented that they would be able to claim extra coal to help dry out their houses.[4]

Flooding at the junction of Melrosegate and Fourth Avenue in Tang Hall in March 1947. This was a year in which severe flooding occurred throughout the city.

(Courtesy of City of York Library)

The author remembers going down Tang Hall Lane to look at the floods after school. Mrs. S. Sykes recalled Melrosegate fields being flooded. She said boats took nearby residents to the shops. Children would often pretend they were going to the shops for their mothers, just to have a ride across the flooded fields.[5]

Local Shops

In the 1940's, there were no big supermarkets in York and people shopped locally. These small shops were very important to local residents and all had their own character. Many people shopped at the Co-operative Stores and looked forward to collecting their "Divvy" money. The local Co-op branch on East Parade was much smaller than today but was well patronised, as was the adjoining butchery department.

The author remembers visiting the local shops on Heworth Road, Heworth Village and East Parade. One of her jobs after school was to pick up the bread from Huitson's off-licence and grocer's shop on Heworth Road. It was always a farmhouse loaf and cost 4½d then. It sat in her basket at the front of her second hand "sit up and beg" bicycle, her treasured possession. However, the crusty top often proved too much temptation and she often had a nibble from the top of the loaf, whilst cycling back home. Once, when she had nibbled too much, her mother was convinced mice had been at the loaf and told her to take it back to the shop. The author, knowing who the real culprit was, refused, but her mother, not to be out done, cycled back to the shop herself. She must have convinced Mrs. Huitson it was mice as she returned home with a spanking new loaf. Next door to Huitson's shop was Mr. Ward's cycle repair shop. He had originally had a workshop down Dale's Lane before moving to Heworth Road. He had a head of thick bushy hair, which was attributed to his habit of running his oily hands through his hair. The author remembers taking accumulators to be recharged at his shop every Saturday morning. These were used for her families' wireless battery set, as there was no electricity laid on where she lived in the 1940's.

Bowerman's fried fish and chip shop, now, Friar Tucks, was well patronised in the 1940's. It was a larger shop then than today and occupied what is now part of the Video Shop. Fish and chips then were a relatively cheap and nourishing meal and there were often long queues outside the shop, especially on a Saturday lunchtime. It was not unusual for people to ask for "one of each" fish 4d, chips 2d, ten or more times. Mr. and Mrs. Jackson worked in this shop for a long time. The Bowerman family who owned this fish shop lived in a house on Heworth Green.

Hargreave's Sweets and Tobacconist occupied the last shop, which is now part of The Video shop and launderette; this shop was very popular with the children.[6]

Mr. North with a trip from the Nag's Head, Heworth. Circa 1950s.

(Courtesy of Miss V. North)

Further along Heworth Road was Mr. North, bookmaker. In the war years this shop sold fruit and vegetables, because all the racing was stopped. However, after the war it was a popular venue for many local men. Mr. North was an amiable man and affectionately known as the "Cock of the North." He was a popular figure on the trips from the Nag's Head, further along Heworth Road.[7]

The Glen Wool shop and Park library along East Parade was a popular venue too. The books all had brightly coloured jackets and could be loaned for 1d or 2d a week. Cobblers and shoe repairers were well patronised in the 1940's as shoes were very expensive to buy. There were three in Heworth, Mr. Deighton near the Co-op. Mr. Singleton in the shop, which is now a branch of Westminster Bank and Mr. Poole on Heworth Green.

Mr. S. Poole remembers his bakery shop in Heworth Village in the 1940's. It was where the flower shop is today. He started work there originally delivering bread and cakes for Mr. and Mrs. Potter, the owners then, but ended up marrying their daughter and after the war took over the running of the shop. His wife did the baking and he was in charge of the deliveries.[8]

The Wireless

Listening to the wireless was one of the most popular pastimes of the 1940's. Many people had Radio Relay installed in their homes which was very cheap. Even if there was no electricity the airways could be picked up with a speaker, battery and accumulators which had to be charged up weekly. Programmes such as "ITMA", "Much Binding in the Marsh" and "Have A Go Joe" with Wilfred Pickles and Violet Carson where very popular. "Children's Hour", "Listen With Mother" and for the older children, " Dick Barton, Special Agent" and "Paul Temple" were the highlights of the week. "Down your Way" and, "Two Way Family Favourites" with Jean Metcalfe and Cliff Mitchelmore and "The Billy Cotton Band Show" were regular popular Sunday shows.

Cinemas

The most popular nightout in the 1940's was a visit to the cinema. In the 1920's and 30's, 2,000 cinemas had been built in Britain and twenty million tickets sold each week. There were small cinemas known locally as "Flea Pits" and the larger grander ones. The latter were often built to look like grand palaces or temples with fake marble columns and chandeliers and statues. The cinema was a great escapism for most working class people. There were always queues outside most cinemas on Saturday nights. The films were shown continually each evening, so if you missed half the main feature, you could sit and wait until it was shown again. The usherettes were always busy showing people to their seats during performances. Having to get up and down to let people pass by, was an unavoidable hazard of cinemas in the 1940's. The Commissionaire was always very grand in his uniform and listening to him shouting the spare seats "One at 1/9" and "2 at 1/-" and to be able to beat the queues was a regular occurrence. In 1945, at the Picture House in Coney Street you could see Diana Durbin and Gene Kelly in "Christmas Holiday", Betty Grable, John Payne and Victor Mature at the Odeon in "Moonlight Serenade" and Budd Abbott and Lou Costello at the St. George's cinema. In 1947, John Mills and Valerie Hobson were in "Great Expectations" at the Odeon, Phyllis Calvert and Stewart Granger in "The Magic Bow" at the Regal and Ann Zeigler, Webster Booth in "Lilac Time "at the Regent. There were nine cinemas in York in the 1940's. In 1948, a special film was shown at the Odeon, sponsored by the Baby Welfare Council called, "The Birth of a Baby", but no one under 18 was allowed entry. Some cinemas like the Clifton Cinema were regular Sunday meeting places for teenagers. Edward Farley played the organ in the interval, but apart from good-natured banter and chatter there was hardly any fights or unruliness.

Home Entertainment

Most people, especially families with young children made their own entertainment at home. Knitting, sewing and crocheting were very popular with the ladies. It was cheaper then to knit woollens and sew your own clothes than to buy ready made. Most girls had to learn to "Make Do and Mend". Clothes were altered to fit younger children and collars and cuffs that had frayed were turned inside out. Sheets and towels were also patched until completely worn out. New materials, such as moygashel and patterned winceyette appeared in the shops after the war. Shops such as Boyes, Renders and Leak and Thorp, that sold materials and dress patterns were very well patronised at this time. Model making and joinery work was popular with the men and boys. In the summer months, gardening was a popular hobby. Most people took a pride in their gardens then and it was rare to see a neglected garden. Council house tenants were especially proud of their gardens. Men who hadn't gardens often took an allotment to grow their own flowers and vegetables. Flower and vegetable shows were the highlights of the gardening year. Many men also kept rabbits, budgies, canaries and pigeons. Fur and Feather shows were very popular too.

Children's Pastimes

Most children made their own entertainment in the home. There were more toys available after the war. Girls enjoyed playing with china dolls, or a dolls' house and tea sets. They often made dolls' clothes and knitted gloves and mittens and made raffia bags out of cardboard milk bottle tops. They loved collecting scraps, (small highly coloured pictures) and swapping them with friends. All children collected cigarette cards and played with marbles and whips and tops. However, most days, children would play outside and mothers could let them roam without fear for their safety from being attacked or molested. Climbing trees, fishing for tiddlers in the becks and playing rounders or cricket were popular with both girls and boys. Girls liked playing hopscotch and skipping games, even boys would often join in a skipping game in the street under a long washing line. In the dark evenings, reading was a popular pastime, Enid Bylton stories, Arthur Ransome's "Swallows and Amazons" series, "Biggles" and school stories were just some of children's childhood favourites.[9]

Mr. D. Reeder's Memories
Mr. Reeder remembers as a boy, climbing trees along Tang Hall beck and riding his bicycle in Heworth streets. He played cricket on the flatter areas of the stray in what seemed to be endless hot summer days. He recalled playing tennis in Glen Park and Burnholme Club grounds and gossiping with friends at street corners and around the seat opposite Bowerman's fish shop.

When he became a teenager, he remembers going to a Youth Club. Here you could try numerous activities and be involved in different types of sport. He recalled many evenings spent at Gleneagles Youth Club, which was held at Tang Hall school and also in a hut on Melrosegate playing fields. The leader then was Mr. Russell Betts. There was also a Youth Club in Heworth. The leader was Mr. R. Taylor.[10]

Mr. Newbald's Memories
Mr. Newbald lived in Clarke's Terrace in the 1940's. He remembers playing football and cricket at the end of his street, near Pulleyn's fields. He recalled a neighbour, Mr. Griffiths, an undertaker, who had a shed on wasteland in Dale's Lane where he made the coffins. The shed is still there he stated and also the board that was shaped to stand the coffins on. He remembers also Mr. Stone, who kept hens on that patch of waste land, and Mr. Hoyes who kept bees. He remembers a Mr. and Mrs. Redhead who managed the chemist' shop near the chapel. They would tell his mother when glucose sweets and Horlick tablets were in the shop to supplement their sweet ration. He also remembers the Britannia when it was a public house and the Wilson family, who lived next door in the large house, Trentholme. Mr. G. Wilson was a painter and decorator.

He attended Heworth School in the 1940's. He recalled a Miss Pratt, Miss Morritt and the Headmaster, Mr. Hepptonstall, who lived then in a flat at the end of Heworth Village. He also remembers the Conservative Hall "down the snicket", connecting Heworth Village to Heworth Hall Drive. It is now a church for the Seventh Day Adventist. The big house at the bottom end of the village, now called Lealholme, was once the home of the Pybus family. Mr. Newbald recalled that it was surrounded by lots of trees and an orchard when he was young. There was also some small cottages near this house occupied by the Smith, Scott and Banford families and workshops in Bland's yard.[11]

The Author's Memories

During the 1940's, the author lived in a wooden bungalow, situated with a few other bungalows, overlooking Monk Stray called Monk Avenue. This bungalow, which was the only accommodation available when her family moved from Hull during the war years, was part of a two family bungalow and had minimal mod cons. There was no electricity laid on and they used gas mantles, which were always breaking, to read by. Cooking was done on a old fashioned range, which her mother regularly blackleaded. There was no bathroom, but there was a bath, which had to be filled from a gas copper in the kitchen. As this bath also doubled up as a table, most baths were taken in a tin bath in front of the fire. The author remembers having to spit on the flat iron to gauge if it was hot enough for ironing and the problems of keeping smuts off the clothes.

However, having the Stray in front of the house and long gardens to play in, made up for the lack of conveniences. Hens and rabbits were kept in the sheds and big barns behind the bungalow and there were always day old chicks at Easter. During the war years ducks and geese were also kept. There was always a plentiful supply of vegetables grown lovingly by the author's father. Tomatoes were regularly cultivated in a greenhouse, which had been transported piece by piece in a wagon from Hull. The author remembers accompanying her father to buy tomato plants from a nursery along Malton Road and calling at the Slip Inn. This pub was very small and she remembers seats outside, practically on the road. This pub was demolished in 1962.

The Stray was just rough pasture in the 1940's, but in the spring it was ablaze with celandines, buttercups and daisies. Wild blue and yellow iris grew at the edges of the pond at the end of Elmfield Terrace. There were smoother areas on the Stray where numerous games of cricket and rounders were played with other children from the Stray bungalows. The Stray was used mostly for pasturing cows and horses then and owned by the Pasture Masters. The Stray master lived in the herdsman's cottage on Malton Road. A large gate prevented the animals from getting into the Monk Avenue bungalows. However this gate was often left open, especially by visitors. Many a night the author remembers being woken up to cries of "Cows Up "and having to get out of bed and help chase the cows from the gardens. Although these bungalows at the side of the Stray were relatively isolated then, the author recalled that she and her brother were always allowed to come home alone, even on dark nights. She remembers crossing the Stray from visiting friends on numerous occasions and all she ever encountered were cows. Tramps would often sleep in the ditch that ran along the side of the Stray but never caused any trouble.

In the other half of the author's bungalow lived the Butler family with two boys. Other families were the Rankin, Hearld, Linfoot, Stockton and Coates families and Mr. & Mrs. Nicholson who moved to No 18 in 1949. The last

Monk Stray, showing the new Manor House. Circa 1940s.

bungalow was occupied by Mr. Amos, the headmaster of the Blue Coat school before its closure in 1946. The Blue Coat school was opened in 1705 in St. Anthony's Hall, Peaseholme Green, for boys of poor freeman of York. In 1938, the school acquired a new playing field at the back of Mr. Amos's bungalow. Mr. Amos had a small farm behind his residence where he kept hens, ducks and pigs. Boys from the Home would regularly come up to the farm to help look after the animals. The author remembers a Blue Coat schoolboy always waiting for her to escort her to Sunday School before returning to Peaseholme Green after doing his chores at the farm. However, after mentioning this to her mother, who must have had a quick word with the Headmaster, the unfortunate boy was relieved of his duties, much to the author's disappointment. She also recalled Bonfire nights with a large bonfire and wonderful fireworks held for the boys in the field behind her bungalow. Access to this field was through two big blue gates in Monk Avenue, now demolished. Later there was a way in from Westland's Grove, Meadow Way. The Blue Coat Old Boys cricket team played on that field after the school closed. Mr. Ernest Webster, a former Blue Coat boy was very much involved with this team and cut and looked after the grass for the matches. His wife organised teas in the old pavilion on the field. Mr. Webster's son, Ronald, played cricket for this team in the 1940's and early 50's. He met the author as he made his way to cricket practice. Later they were married, until his untimely death from cancer in 1989. When the Old Boy's cricket team was disbanded in 1955, Heworth Cricket team leased this field. After Heworth had moved to Elmpark Way, a team from Ben Johnson's played here. A modern house for the Blue Coat and Grey Coat schools, amalgamated in 1946, called Stray Garth was erected at the side of this field in the 1960's. The schools closed in the 1990's, and the house is now a home for adults with special needs. The old playing field was sold in 1990 and new houses were built.[12]

Burnholme Working Men's Club

The author's father, Mr. A. T. Reeder, was a member of Burnholme Club in the 1940's. The author remembers going to the Christmas parties there and playing tennis in the grounds. She always went with her parents to see the annual walking match on August Bank Holiday Monday. The winner received "The Flower Cup", presented by the Flower family in memory of William Flower, a former Club Vice President and his son Clarence, who was killed in active service during the war.[13]

The Club had thriving cricket, angling and bowling teams in the 1940's and early 1950's. Mr. Eric Stainsby was the Captain of the cricket team, his brother Fred was the Secretary and Mr. Bert Bonner the President. Percy Reid was the Secretary of the bowls section and the Captain was George Sutton. George Thompson was Secretary of the angling club and Harold Senior the President. Other men involved with the running of the club in these years were Mr. Fred Winter, Mr. E. Clack. Mr. F. Leaper, Mr. Cyril Robertson, Mr. N. Clarke, steward, and the President of the club Mr. T. Sumpton.

Burnholme Club was reputed to be haunted. No committee member would ever venture up into the attic rooms where the ghost of a "White Lady" was said to have been seen. The ghost was reputed to be the mistress of a former owner.[14]

The Shoulder of Mutton

Mr. Laycock remembers his parents running this pub in the 1940's and living there then. He was told it had been built in early Victorian times as a "Tontine". Ten men had put £100 into a fund to buy a house and land, later one man bought them all out. It was also reputed to have been a place where rich Victorian businessmen could meet their lady friends.

In the war years there was a shortage of beer and Mr. Laycock recalled the queues that formed outside the pub when a quota was due. In the men's bar, darts and dominoes were played and there was always a Christmas party. There was a Cricket Club in the 1940's, which played only away games, as it had no home ground. There was also an annual walking match and competitors would have to walk to the Hopgrove and back. In 1955, the licence was moved to No 54 Heworth Green and the old "Shoulder" became a private house again.[15]

The Shoulder of Mutton, no. 74 Heworth Green. This pub closed in 1955 and the licence was transferred to no 64 once called Heworth Hyrst. Circa 1900. (*Courtesy of J Murphy*)

Chapter IX. Notes and References.

1. *Y.E.P.* 1945.
2. *Y.E.P.* 1947.
3. Ibid. 1945-1947.
4. *Y.E.P.* Feb.1947.
5. Information supplied by Mrs. Sykes, Mrs. Appleton.
6. Memories of Author. Mrs. Appleton (née Reeder).
7. Information supplied by Miss V. North, Hempland Avenue.
8. Memories of Mr. S. Poole, Vyner Street.
9. Memories of Author & *Y.E.P.* (1945-1948)
10. Information supplied by Mr. D. Reeder, 17 Chantry Hurst. Epsom.
11. Memories of Mr. Newbald, 91a Heworth Village.
12. Memories of Author and Mr. E. Webster (late Woolnough House).
13. Memories of Author and Mr. A. T. Reeder (late Monk Avenue)
14. *Y. Gazette and Herald.* 2.8.1952.
15. Information supplied by Mr. Laycock, 74a Heworth Green.

CHAPTER X
The New Elizabethan Era

The death of King George VI and the subsequent Coronation of Queen Elizabeth II in 1953, heralded a new Elizabethan Era. Goods were becoming more plentiful, although rationing did not cease until 1953. Sweets had come off rationing in 1949. Many materials for clothes were now available and the "Princess Look" or the "New Look" became very fashionable. Coats and dresses were nipped in at the waist with long full skirts. Frills and flounces of lace were often sown at the bottom of old dresses to be in keeping with the new fashion. Dirnl skirts made from bright new prints and black elasticated belts were very popular at this time. Light sport's jackets and trousers and shirts with attached collars instead of loose ones appeared in the shops for men.[1]

New Housing Developments

In the 1950's, new housing estates were built with houses that young couples could afford to buy. R. Cattle built houses in the Hempland Lane and Hempland Drive areas at a price of around £2,000. Philip Wainhouse purchased land in the Whitby Avenue and Ashley Park area and built his bungalow development. These houses ranged in price from £1,500 - £1,700 and with a deposit of £150, were in the price range of many young couples. The Whitby Avenue Supermarket, owned by Hetherton, Solicitors, was also built at this time. This was the first supermarket in York but was demolished in the 1980's. In 1958/59 the house at the beginning of Dale's Lane was demolished to provide for the widening and extending of this road. The house was rebuild further along Dales Lane. Houses were then built along Hempland Avenue and Oakland Avenue where Paradise Cottage and Pulleyn's fields had once been.[2] Freddy Truman lived in one of these houses for a while in the 1960's.

In 1958, York Corporation took over the maintenance of Monk Stray from the wardens and pasture masters. The Stray was drained and became an open area for the recreation of the public. Each freeman and freeman's widow received a sum of £1 per annum in perpetuity. In the 1970's, flats, which overlooked the Stray were built along Monk Avenue, where once the Manor House gardens had been. The house next to the Manor House, now called Monk Stray House, and the Charles Moor development were built at this time. Tennis courts that belonged to Centenary Chapel had previously been in this area.[3]

Heworth Football Club

Heworth Parish Football club started up in 1897 but disbanded in 1914 because of the war. The team was known then as "The Bantams" as it was customary to take a bantam to matches and place it on the crossbar of the goal posts. The club was started up again in the 1950's by the efforts of Mr. Harry Southwood, Mr. Nettleship and Mr. K. Banks, the latter acting as Secretary. In the 1960's, the team played at the sport's ground at the bottom of Elmpark Way, It was Mr. Southwood's dream to have a multi sport's centre there, with bowling greens, tennis courts and gymnasium. Unfortunately Mr. Southwood died in 1968 before his dream could materialise. Perhaps the new Ryedale Centre is the nearest thing to his dreams.

Heworth Rugby Club

Heworth Rugby Amateur League Club formed in 1922 following a revival in the interest of rugby in York after the Yorks. Cup Final between York and Bramley. In the 1930's junior sides were started and a "base" was secured at the Tang Hall Hotel. In the 1960's the club played on a field near the present Hempland School. In the 1950's and 60's the club achieved numerous successes in local cup competitions following Heworth's acceptance to the Leeds and District League. Many players gained County and International honours and the club had the distinction of winning the Yorkshire under 21 Cup in 1950/51 and 1951/52.

Heworth went on to become York's leading club and in the 1970's acquired it's own ground and clubhouse at Elmpark way. Since then there has been extensions to the clubhouse and changing facilities, a covered stand, ground drainage and floodlights.

Over the years two hundred players have signed professional forms. The most notable being Geoff Wrigglesworth (Leeds), Ken Bowman (Huddersfield), Colin Forsyth (Oldham), David Watkinson (Hull Kingston Rovers), and Gary Divorty (Hull). In more recent times Chris Hammerton played for York R.L.C. and Ken Sykes had twelve years with Hunslet R.L.F.C.[4]

Heworth Cricket Club

A strip of parchment exists in the Castle Museum containing the rules of the York area's first cricket club, drawn up in 1784. This stated that all those whose names were on the charter had agreed to meet on Heworth Moor every Tuesday and Friday morning at 4am to play cricket. They also agreed to pay 1d a game and to be fined 3d if not within sight of the wickets before the Minster struck 5 a.m. Both York Cricket Club and Heworth Cricket Club claim the distinction of being associated with this early spartan existence. As the original parchment was signed by prominent Heworth residents it seems likely that the charter marked the formation of an early Heworth Club. However York Cricket Club did play on Heworth Moor from 1784-1791 before they moved to the Knavesmire.[5]

The old Heworth parish cricket club was formed in Victorian times. In the 1920's the team played on Herbert's Fields down Stockton Lane, then in the 1930's on Scobey's Fields which was near the Vicarage.

In 1937, the team consisted of T. Baram, H. Barnit, N. Bean (Captain), W. Beavers, W. Berry, W. Cooper, F. Dennis, J. Everitt, R. W. Inspear, B. king, H. Lazenby, G. Lee, V. Pattison, Mr. Thompson, H. Watkinson and T. Williams.[6]

Mrs. J. Southwood remembers the team playing on a field near Hempland Lane. She recalled herself and Pat Cable going in a taxi to the Creamery Cafe in Pavement to collect flasks of tea to give to the players.[7] In 1950 there were five cricket teams in Heworth, Blue Coat Old Boy's, Burnholme, Heworth, Muncaster Tenants Association, and the Shoulder of Mutton. By 1954 there was only Heworth Cricket Club still in existence, This team, with many new members from the other clubs, played on the old Blue Coat School playing field at Meadow Way. This field ran along the back of the Monk Avenue bungalows. In 1958, D. J. Holmes topped the 1st X1 League and Cup batting averages whilst B Sutcliffe headed the bowling. A. Martindale led the overall batting averages that year. The 2nd X1 League and Cup batting averages was topped by J. Dunnington and the bowling by C. Armstrong and E. Lawson. The chairman was Councillor J. M. Wood and Vice Chairman, H. P. Southwood. Mr. C. Elliker was the Secretary assisted by S. Sanders and B. Carter. The 1st X1 Captain was H. J. Thomas, Vice-Captain E Wrighton and the 2nd X1, Captain, N. Bean and Vice-Captain R. B. Webster.

Other men involved with the Club in these early days were T. Baram, L. Cooper, F. Powell, D. Kilvington E. Turner, T. Williams and D. Wilson. In 1964 the Club moved to a playing field at the bottom of Elmpark Way and shared a ground and clubhouse with York Hockey Club. In the 1960's and 1970's the Club grew and expanded and there were three adult teams then. M. Caddie, R. Carrington, A. Carter, T. Fannan, E. A. Fryth, D. Inns, K. Johnnson, S. Johnnson, I. Machell, K. C. Matthews, T. G. Raines, I. Reid and D. Wragg, were just some of the men who helped Heworth to become the successful cricket club it is today. Over the years over 1,000 players have been registered with Heworth so there are many more players who could have been mentioned. Today the Club has four adult teams and two junior teams and is one of the leading cricket clubs in York. Noel Bean has been associated with the club since the 1930's and now acts as groundsman. Cliff Elliker joined the Club in 1951, acted as secretary for more than 25 years and is still very involved with the running of the club.[8]

Heworth Tennis Club

Heworth Tennis Club, which is situated on East Parade, was originally called the Parade Tennis Club. It appears to have been in existence since the early years of this century. Mrs. Southwood, who lived in Second Avenue as a girl, remembers going to watch the tennis with her parents in the 1920's.

There was another tennis club in Heworth at this time called Heworth Tennis Club. This was situated where Hyrst Grove is now, at the back of the big house on Heworth Green, once called Heworth Grange, now a doctor's surgery. The Wright family, who were butchers in York, owned this land before the War.

After the War this club was reformed with some members that had played at the Parade Club. However in the 1950's, the land on which the tennis club stood was sold to Mr. H. Williamson, builder. The members were given notice to quit.

After this club closed some of the members returned to the Parade Club. This was then owned by York Telephone Area Sports and Social Club and leased by York Police Tennis Club.

In the mid 1950's, because of lack of interest by the former clubs, the tennis club was reformed with a new committee and trustees and renamed Heworth Tennis Club. Mr. B. Kendall and Mr. P. Shepherd are two surviving original trustees from these days. Mr. G. Davies, the present president was involved with the old tennis club on Heworth Green in the 1940's and the one on East Parade since the re-organisation in the 1950's.[9]

Heworth Golf Club

The first meeting to form a Golf Club was held on 30th March 1911, in a room in the new Rifle Range at the bottom of Harcourt Street. The first committee consisted of A. M. Wiseley, N. Sharp, T. Masser, T. Thompson and F. Murray. H. V. Rymer of East Parade and Mr. Slack the Headmaster of Elmfield College were other early members. There was also three lady members. The course consisted of fifteen acres of land on Heworth Moor, that belonged to Mr. Moiser of Heworth Grange and fifteen acres of the brickfields. The first rules stated that there had to be a minimum of eighty gentlemen to form a club and the annual subsciption would be £1-11-6d. It was also agreed to obtain the services of a Strensall professional to supervise the laying out of the links. At another meeting held at the home of the secretary, Mr. J.A. Foster 12 Second Avenue, the committee agreed to have their own professional, Mr. H. Gammon, and to employ a groundsman at a weekly wage of a £1. The annual subscription was to be £1-1s for men,£1-11-6d for women and juniors 10-6d. Caddies would cost 4d per round, 3d of this money was for cleaning the clubs and 1d for insurance. The Hon Francis Jackson was elected the first President and Major Simpson and Mr. Stewart, Vice-Presidents.

The first clubhouse, a portable building costing £57, was erected in the west corner of the present Golf course near the bend of Pottery Lane. This had been the site of an old pottery. The first course consisted of seven tees and six greens. Heworth Golf Club was officially opened in 1912 but the ceremony was delayed due to bad weather. These early golfers encountered many hazards on their way around the course. They had to pass Mr. Walker's brickyards and ponds, a private rifle range and a clay pigeon shoot.Cattle and sheep regularly grazed on the links.An agreement had been made with the Pasture Masters of Monk Stray that the Club would be held responsible for any damage to stock. In these early days horses were used to pull the grass cutters but were often allowed to stray away from the golf course.On one occasion one horse had fallen into a pond and one had wandered far away, became lost and had frozen to death. In 1933, the Club decided to lease Muncaster House as a clubhouse. The previous owner had been Mr. Denby Collins, a builder. Since that time there has been alterations to the clubhouse and extensions to the course.

Today the Club has a 12 hole course and 450 members. It is one of the oldest in York and a founder member of the Y.U.C.G. Until 1988 it was the only club within the York boundary.

Public Houses

The Britannia public house closed in the 1960's, the last landlords were the Haithwaite family. The licence was then transferred to the Walnut Tree. This house had been offices for Bass Charington Breweries since the 1950's. Mr. V. Coulson was the first landlord. He had previously been the landlord of the Beehive, Doncaster. The licence for the Shoulder of Mutton public house on Heworth Green moved in 1952 to the big house No 64, at the corner of Cinder Lane and the old pub became a private house again. In 1970, the house next to the old Shoulder became a hotel, Heworth Court Hotel.[10]

Heworth Moor House

Heworth Moor House still continued as a home for unmarried mothers until the 1980's. In 1960, the Home was run by Mrs. Addison, the widow of a Suffolk clergyman. Illegitimacy was still a disgrace in those days and to avoid scandal among the neighbours, unmarried pregnant girls were sent away to Homes in other towns. It cost £7 a week to keep a girl at Heworth Moor House in the 1960's. There was no state aid, only the girl's maternity benefit. Sometimes the parents of the mother would help, and occasionally those of the fathers. The girls would stop at the Home for twelve weeks, six before and six weeks after the birth. The fathers were not allowed to visit the girls in the Home and most babies were adopted. There was also a chapel in the basement so that babies could be baptised. "These girls were not bad girls but perhaps unfortunate, weak and a little foolish", commented the Matron in 1961. Many of the fathers were married men, and incest was a common occurrence. Because in the 1980's unmarried mothers were more accepted by society and could afford to keep their babies, the Home eventually closed.[11]

Changes in the Village

On Heworth Road the old North Riding Police Station closed in the 1950's and became Fannon's taxi business and a bookies shop. Granger's plumbers moved into the yard next to the Nag's Head. Hudson's butcher's shop opened in 1961 and Miss Bristow had her milk business at the corner of Heworth Road.

Three cottages at the end of Heworth village were demolished in the 1950's, and alms houses built along Hempland Lane near the beck. Mr. Chapman opened his garage in 1960 and flats were later built at the back of Bland's Yard, called Glaisby Court. Hildreth House became offices for Sorrell's builders, and Brumfitts, the plumbers, moved into the White House. Two houses at the end of Heworth Road were demolished in 1970 to widen the corner. Les-Lee occupied the shop that had once been Miss Walker's haberdashery. Mr. North's shop became a hairdresser's shop in the 1970's and next door was Mr. Hudson's butcher's shop. Mr. Hudson had previously had a shop near Monk Bar.[12]

In 1969 Mr. & Mrs. K Evans opened a laundrette in the old sweet shop, once Hargeaves, then Doherty's shop. The fish shop became Friar Tucks with a vegetable section managed by Mr. T Williams. In the 1980's Mr. Evans bought this vegetable section and enlarged his shop and started his video department. This was known as the Ace Video and Laundrette. Friar Tuck's fish and chip shop was reduced in size and was situated at one end of the block. Mr. & Mrs. Evans came to live in the village at the old Britannia Inn, then a private house, in 1975.[13]

Some of the garden belonging to the big house Trentholme, now called The Coach House, was sold in 1970 and a new mews development was built. This was aptly named Mulwith Close, in memory of Mary Ward, who had been born at Mulwith, near Ripon. In the 1990's, new Methodist old people's homes, Field Court, was built in the Hempland Lane area of Heworth Village.

The kiosk in the old electric bus shelter at the top of Stockton Lane closed in the 1980's and was due to be demolished. However it was bought by Mrs. A Turner and opened as a flower shop. This shop still has the old posts engraved with the initials of many courting couples who had frequented the bus shelter. The author remembers the shelter, it was a popular meeting place for teenagers in the late 1940s. Lads from Clifton Cycling Club would often congregate here after their weekly runs. However there was never any trouble, fights or vandalism.

In the 1950's, The Limes became a hostel for St. John's College and no 108 Heworth Green, offices for the River Board. This changed to the headquarters of the Girl Guides in the 1970's. The old N.E.R. laundry was demolished in the 1970's and sheltered housing built down Dodsworth Avenue. Heworth Grange became a convent for St. Wilfrid's then, but today it is a doctor's surgery. Wheatley's Garage became Chrystal Garage and Foster's provision shop, Dykes. It is now an insurance agent's shop.[14]

Further Changes

Burnholme School, later renamed Burnholme Community College, was opened in 1950 in Bad Bargain Lane, and in 1983 'Galtres', a school for children with special needs was built. In 1962 a new branch library, welfare clinic and a Catholic school for girls, Margaret Clitheroe's were opened in Fifth Avenue, Tang Hall. It is now St. Aelred's Primary School.

A road over the Osbaldwick Beck, Stray Road was built in the late 1960's, which joined Apple Tree Village to the Ashley Park and Whitby Avenue housing estates A community centre was built in that area in the 1980's. Hempland School was opened in 1969 in Whitby Avenue, the first Headmaster was Mr. Wain. A bungalow was demolished in Whitby Drive and new houses built in Caedmon Close. The Whitby Avenue supermarket was demolished in the early years of 1990 and new shops, maisonettes and a doctor's surgery built.[15]

Heworth Today

Heworth today, although now a suburb of York, still retains some of its village characteristics. The village school is still in use and London's shop, Woods Chemists, Newton's hairdresser's and the Co-op are still flourishing in spite of new out of town shopping developments such as Monk's Cross.

The church and chapel are still well attended although in keeping with modern trends, not as much as they used to be. A new church, Christ Church, was built along Stockton Lane in 1960 to cater for the residents of the Ashley Park and Greenfield Park housing development. Today the church and chapel often hold joint services. They both try and bring their teachings in line with modern society and endeavour to be of service to all people, who are in any kind of need. They offer families, services and social events, Mums and small children creches and playgroups and for older children, scouts and guides, choir and youth clubs. They also organise social activities and services for adults, the elderly, house bound and infirm.[16]

As the new Millennium approaches, the author hopes that this book will help people recall and remember former inhabitants of Heworth, who have played their part, however small, in shaping Heworth and making it the pleasant suburb it is today.

Avril E. Webster Appleton.

Chapter X. Notes and References.

1. *Y.E.P.* 1948-1953.
2. Y.C.A. *Y.C.C. Minutes.* 1950-1970.
3. Memories of Mrs. Crawshaw, Hempland Avenue. *Y.C.C. Minutes* (1950-1970)
4. Information supplied by Mrs. Southwood, Mr. Sykes, Heworth Rugby.
5. Information supplied by Mr. C. Elliker, 15 Walney Road.
6. Information supplied by Mr. N. Bean, 1 Bean's Way.
7. Memories. Mrs. Southwood.
8. Information supplied by Mr. C. Elliker.
9. Information supplied by Mr. G. Davies, Stockton Lane.
10. *Minutes of Heworth Golf Club.*
11. *Y.E.P.* 19.10.1965. 1950-1952.
12. *Y.C.C. Minutes.* 1950-1970.
13. Information supplied by Mr. K. Evans, 70-72 Heworth Village.
14. *Y.C.C. Minutes.* 1950-1970.
15. Ibid. 1970-1990.
16. Heworth Church & Chapel. *Newsletter.* 1999.

Sports Day at Melrosegate Playing Fields to celebrate the Coronation, 1953.

(Courtesy of J. Nelson)

Kellys 1949/50. Reproduced from Kellys Street Directory 1949/50. *(Courtesy of Kellys)*

Fosters grocer's shop occupied the corner of East Parade and Mill Lane from the 1890's to the 1950's.

Mr. C G Wheatley's shop and Garage in Mill Lane, circa 1960's. Tow houses (Sister Wilson's House) that once stood next to the shop were demolished in the 1950's. Hainsworth's Off-Licence was knocked down in the 1970's to extend the forecourt of Crystal Motorist Centre.

V.E. Party outside the Walnut Tree House 1945.

(Courtesy of Mrs. Murray)

Heworth Conservative Club outing. Circa 1930s.

Heworth Cricket Club. Married v Singles 1957.

Back Row: C Armstrong. R Clarke. H Southwood. G Asher. C J Dunnington. J Pennock. J Stubbs. E Lawson.

Middle Row: E Turner. A Martindale. F Dennis. F Powell. S Saunders. B Sutcliffe. D Wilson. D R Bruce. D Miller. N Bean.

Front Row: D Kilvington. C Elliker. A J Thomas. T Baram. E Wrighton. R B Webster.

(Courtesy of The Evening Press York)

94

INDEX OF PLACES

97